MW00773125

Praise for *The Proactive Executive*

"Careers are a personal journey of discovery, Chris Nadherny's book, The Proactive Executive, provides an exceptional map for understanding the actions, decisions, market positioning and personal development that ultimately determine whether we have effectively managed our careers or fallen short of 'what could have been'. His book is one that should certainly be read sooner rather than later!"
—*John Koryl, President, Neiman Marcus Stores & Online*

"Having read and prescribed many career books, this would be my absolute top choice. The author's perspective is unique in that his vast executive search experience provides insight both from a company's view as well as from the prospective executive. Together, they form a mosaic of what really defines exceptional talent and how this should guide one's career decisions. Chris Nadherny has created a career management reference guide that will prove invaluable for many aspiring executives in the years to come."
—*Fred Ley, SVP Corporate HR and Global Talent Management and Acquisition, Walmart, Inc.*

"In 'Proactive Executive' Chris Nadherny has consolidated his decades of learnings in the executive search business to create an invaluable blueprint for optimizing your career. His book is packed full of insights, practical how-to's and suggestions for aspiring C-suite professionals. The lessons that he shares are particularly relevant in today's ultra-competitive marketplace."
—*Jody Bilney, SVP and Chief Consumer Officer, Humana, Inc.*

"Chris Nadherny shares his considerable experience as a national C-suite recruiter to capture the most critical, but often overlooked, elements of professional development and career planning in his book, "The Proactive Executive." His book is full of proven and practical advice, insights, how-to's, action steps and real life case studies to guide your journey. A great read!"
—*Kimberly Williams, CEO, Consumer Safety Technologies*

"Today as you move up an organization or change companies in a leadership position, you need the total package. Chris Nadherny outlines the steps needed to prepare yourself in advance for a significant career move, and to make sure it is the right one. Importantly, his approach makes these difficult steps achievable."
—Roger Adams, Chief Marketing Officer, Fortune 500 diversified financial services company, Board Member, Association of National Advertisers.

"Want help in improving your career? Then read this book before it's too late. Chris Nadherny turns 30 years of executive search experience into a reference guide that offers invaluable advice for executives at every stage of their careers."
—Gian Fulgoni, Co-Founder & CEO at comScore, Inc.

"Read this book! No fluff here. Only practical tools and 'hard' career management skills that are guaranteed to result in positive career and personal growth. This is a 'go to' resource successful executives can pick up throughout their careers."
—John Seebeck, VP and General Manager ECommerce, CDW, Inc.

"Physician heal thyself hasn't typically been relevant advice for business executives. Until now. Chris Nadherny's 'Proactive Executive' does just that. This book reminds smart, strategic, and effective executives, who have mastered goal setting, planning, execution and monitoring, to apply these very talents to managing their own careers. Starting with the most important trait, self-awareness, Chris brings evidence in the form of examples and cases proving the qualities, and then the strategic actions that he's seen work over a stellar career of his own in executive search."
—Tom Collinger, Executive Director Medill IMC/Spiegel Digital and Database Research Initiative, Northwestern University

"I have known Chris for nearly 20 years as a candidate, client and friend. This book powerfully distills career management insights from the thirty year career of someone I consider to be one of the world's most respected search executives. The detailed case studies, what-if scenarios, lessons learned and proactive action plans he lays out will be invaluable to executives at any stage in their career."
—Love Goel, CEO, GVG Capital

the Proactive Executive

Executive

A C-Suite Recruiter's 5-Step System for Achieving Greater Career Success

by Chris Nadherny

…

Distributed by Bublish, Inc.
bublish.com

…

Cover design by AM Design Studios

…

Page design and layout by Tasha Kenyon

…

ISBN-10: 1-946229-55-5
ISBN-13: 978-1-946229-55-7

The Proactive Executive, my first book, is dedicated to my late father and my mother (still kicking!), both incredibly loving and supportive role models. My father passed on to me his energy, enthusiasm for life, drive, integrity and love of people. I recall him telling me, more times than I can remember, "You are no better than anyone else...but, damn it, nobody else is better than you!" I inherited from my mother her creativity, what charm I possess, and at least part of her ability to carry on a conversation with almost anyone. As a couple, Mom and Dad had a magical gift for truly engaging with others. They were connectors. I will always marvel at the breadth and richness of their friendships...and their resilience and patience in raising a family of five children, all born within a span of only seven years...that was a lot of cloth diapers on any given day!

Table of Contents

Introduction

Over the course of my 30 years with Spencer Stuart, a leading global executive search firm, I had the unique opportunity to meet and assess thousands of successful executives. As a consultant and partner, I engaged in more than 700 senior executive search assignments for a wide range of small, mid-sized, large and global client organizations, both public and privately held. My efforts on behalf of these client companies spanned across multiple industries and job functions at levels ranging from vice president to chief executive officer and board director roles. These interactions provided me with invaluable insights about what successful careers look like and how they are formed.

I also observed the missteps taken by many bright, well-educated and energetic executives. For the most part, these missteps were avoidable—the result of poor decisions, improper career planning and insufficient career management. Lack of effective career management almost always has a detrimental impact on an executive's career advancement, job satisfaction, and earnings potential. Yet, so often, promising professionals don't have the career guidance or broader real-world perspective that are so beneficial. That is why, after retiring from Spencer Stuart in 2015, I set about writing a practical, actions-based reference book to help aspiring and C-suite executives optimize their career management. This discipline has not, for the most part, been taught by our education system at any level. Instead, we painfully learn these lessons through the school of hard knocks.

My vision for this book is to share the most helpful insights and observations I have gained about effective career management as well as offer honest, insightful and straightforward guidance to prevent executives from wasting their potential due to career mismanagement or inattention to personal and professional development. The result is *The Proactive Executive: A C-Suite Recruiter's 5-Step System for Achieving Greater Career Success*.

I believe that two-thirds of professional success is controllable. When executives are proactive, aware, informed and understand effective career-management practices, they can mitigate or eliminate costly professional missteps. *The Proactive Executive* provides a proven framework for *optimizing* career potential. For some, this may mean ascending the career ladder. For others, it may revolve around meaning and mission or be defined within the context of being a single parent or raising a family. The insights, ideas and suggestions offered in the pages of this book will have a positive impact on your career, no matter what your aspirations.

The Proactive Executive provides real-life case studies and learnings from executives I've known and with whom I've worked closely. Ultimately, the success of their careers was linked to the attractiveness of their executive profile—specifically, their unique combination of skills, knowledge, experience, and interpersonal abilities. By the time you finish this book, you will have a solid understanding of how to more effectively manage your career and build a compelling executive profile. You will:

- Grasp the relevance of supply and demand in the talent market
- Know the most important selection criteria that employers assess
- Be able to judge the current attractiveness of your executive profile
- Apply a practical system for assessing your professional strengths and limitations
- Understand how to create a compelling resume, crush job interviews, and work with a search firm
- Be able to apply the ten key building blocks of successful career management

For more resources and information about how to build a successful career, visit my website, chrisnadherny.com. Let's get started!

1

STEP ONE

Establish a Proactive Mindset
Toward Your Career

"I believe that everyone chooses how to approach life. If you're proactive, you focus on preparing. If you're reactive, you end up focusing on repairing." — *John C. Maxwell*

|||||

You are the CEO of your career. No one will ever care more about your career than you do. Even if you have a personal board of advisors and mentors, ultimately the buck stops with you. The decisions you make throughout your career, the actions you take or avoid, your self-awareness of your assets and liabilities, your receptiveness to feedback, and your ability to establish a powerful and differentiated professional brand—all of these crucial career building elements are controlled by you.

While some successful careers unfold largely by happenstance or luck, very few of us are so fortunate. Establishing a game plan and career objectives that match your skills and interests is a much more reliable route to success. This approach maps out the skill sets and experiences you'll need to acquire in order to achieve those objectives. As your career evolves, you can update your game plan to reflect emerging market needs and skill requirements, new interests, and opportunities not previously considered.

The one thing you can count on during your forty or more years of work is constant change. The pace of change in the business world has never been greater. The vitality of organizations and their employees careers are shaped by multiple, ever-shifting forces—global competition, the health of regional and world economies, consumption trends, monetary policies, global politics and rapid advances in technology. In today's business environment, you cannot afford to be a passive observer. Like any great CEO, you must take charge. You must be proactive. All too often, however, I have watched professionals let their careers "happen" to them without taking time for proper reflection and forethought. In some ways, this mindset is not entirely surprising. Up until the point when we embarked on our careers, most of us were pulled through an educational system that told us which courses to take, what books to read, when to be in class, when to take exams, and so on. Though we applied ourselves to the task at hand, we became accustomed to the predictability of this environment. Educators had little or no time to prepare us for the unruliness of the real world or encourage us to think about the bigger picture—who we are, what we are good at, and where we want to go.

> Educators had little or no time to prepare us for the unruliness of the real world . . .

I've met a number of executives who have carried this passive mindset into their careers. They become comfortable in a role or at a company and fail to consider the importance of growing—continually enriching and shaping their backgrounds. "I'm being paid reasonably," they tell themselves, "My job is fine. I feel secure." In other cases, professionals become so busy "doing" their jobs that they fail to reflect upon where their career is headed. Admittedly, there may be times when you accept that your career is going to move at a more measured pace to accommodate short-term circumstances. One example of this is when a family has children in school and does not want to disrupt their education and friendships. However, to be stuck in this mode, whether intentionally or unintentionally, will limit your career development.

Reactive Versus Proactive

To demonstrate the impact mindset can have on your career, let's take a look at the career paths of two executives. Their stories will help us better understand the dynamics and outcomes associated with a passive approach versus a proactive one. Though their names have been changed, both stories are real.

I met Sara in 2015. A very bright female executive with top-tier academic credentials, she started her career in a highly respected general-management consulting firm after receiving her MBA. Well-spoken, energetic, articulate, and hardworking, Sara was intensely focused on the task at hand—client engagements and meeting her delivery deadlines. She was very loyal to her firm and took little time to reflect on her long-term professional game plan and development...or consider how her skill sets could be applied to different types of roles in the market. After eight years with her employer, the firm decided to spin off several businesses, including her practice area. Sara was caught off-guard and quickly accepted a similar role with another general management consulting firm without properly considering alternative opportunities. This new role, similar to her prior one, offered limited opportunity to develop new skill sets or demonstrably different experiences. Additionally, her background was not terribly unique from other consultants in this new firm. As a result, when the economy took a downturn a year later, she was not viewed as essential to the business and was let go. Through a prior colleague's connection, Sara was then introduced to a marketing-research firm where she accepted a key client-service role. Her consulting and client-service skills were valued at this firm. Unfortunately, the company was acquired by a private equity firm and went into cost-cutting mode. Not wanting

> She was very loyal to her firm and took little time to reflect on her long-term professional game plan . . .

to be part of this, Sara decided to return to the more familiar general-management consulting path with a second tier organization where she stayed for another two years before recognizing that the firm's primary focus was outside her area of expertise. She then moved on to an even smaller consulting firm that had a primary focus outside her area of expertise but which desired to expand into sectors she was familiar with. Ultimately, this firm's commitment to expansion diminished and Sara has found it challenging to obtain the resources required to build a new practice. She has continued with this firm but is not finding it to be very satisfying.

After multiple rapid career moves that did not add demonstrable market value to her background, Sara finally stopped to take a look at the bigger picture. In hindsight, it became clear to her that she would have benefited significantly from a more proactive game plan much earlier in her career. This plan would have helped her grow further skill sets, experiences and achievements to build a stronger and more differentiated market position. Stronger market positioning—a result of more acute self-reflection and better researched career decisions—would likely have resulted in a much better situation midway through her career.

Without a long-term career plan, Sara was reactive rather than strategic in her job choices. Her career moves did little to build a recognized and valued set of competencies. As a result, instead of being able to manage her career from a position of strength, she found it necessary to compromise on the quality and stability of the organizations with which she became affiliated. Her moves to less stable and less satisfying work environments further exacerbated her professional challenges. Had Sara envisioned how her strengths could play broadly across multiple industry sectors, she could have expanded the array of opportunities for which she could be considered and made more deliberate job decisions.

Contrast Sara's story with another bright executive, Mike, who commenced his career in marketing with a highly regarded consumer goods company for several years before returning to school for his MBA. He then spent four years with a top tier general-management consulting firm before returning to his former consumer goods employer and progressing to the role of marketing director. Mike then moved out of his comfort zone to become a brand-marketing director at a large technology company and then cofounded an ecommerce company that was sold to Amazon. It was clear early on that Mike liked taking on new challenges and diving into new experiences. Mike then moved to a rapidly growing, recognized west coast online marketplace business where he progressed to the title of Senior Vice President of Marketing within six years. After learning as much as he could there, he jumped out of his comfort zone once again to take on the role of CEO at a smaller company in the payments

> **Mike liked taking on new challenges and diving into new experiences.**

processing arena. The company needed significant revitalization, which Mike was able to deliver. With his accomplishments and career on the rise, Mike next took what some might consider an unconventional step *down* the corporate ladder. He became Vice President of Consumer Marketing for a rapidly growing Internet search and ad platform that was experiencing rapid growth. With this valuable experience under his belt, he was recruited three years later to be Chief Marketing Officer of a recognized, global online social platform. While many careers do not involve this many company moves, each of Mike's transitions added valuable experience and dimensions to his profile and positioned him in growth sectors. His accomplishments and track record were amplified by his ability to identify high growth scenarios where his skill sets were highly valued. He was also willing to accept some calculated risk in entering these high growth scenarios.

Mike, unlike Sara, built key foundational skills and competencies across marketing, branding, strategy, and general management. He identified and was open to opportunities to take on new challenges that allowed him to transition his skill sets into other industry sectors, larger and smaller companies, growth and turn-around scenarios. He shaped his profile for the emerging digital environment. He jumped on the early growth curve of the Internet and identified opportunities where he knew he could make a dif-ference. He accumulated experience across line and staff roles in multiple industry sectors. He gained valuable general management experience and perspective while also broadening his marketing skill sets. With each move, Mike further differentiated his skill sets and experience in the marketplace. He sought out opportunities in the Internet space to make his background more contextually relevant to the rapidly emerging demands of the talent market. Importantly, he built a reputation for making a positive impact. The varied skill sets and experiences he has accumulated throughout his career position him to be considered for an attractive array of opportunities in the future.

To recap, let's do a side-by-side comparison of both Sara and Mike's careers.

Sara	Mike
No real game plan	Game plan, but open to modification
Passive mindset	Proactive mindset
More limited skill sets	Built range of skill sets
Reactive job changes	Deliberate job changes
Limiting career decisions	Expansive career decisions
Stayed within her comfort zone	Sought out new growth opportunities

How to Develop a Proactive Mindset for Your Career

We've clearly seen the difference that having a proactive versus reactive mindset can make in a career. Given that you are an educated professional in an executive level role—and reading this book—I presume you have a desire to more proactively manage your career. Your issue is not motivation, but education—a gap in understanding how to go about this. Here's how to begin:

- **Stop and self-reflect:** Find quiet, uninterrupted intervals to think back through your entire background from a young age to the present. Look for instances and patterns of those 2-3 things that you have done well repeatedly, and that tend to come naturally to you. Add 2-3 recognized skill sets that you have built, either through education or on the job learning. Now, overlay these skills with your interests—several things about which you are passionate. Determine how these three components—natural talents, learned skills, and passions—overlap with your current company and industry, if possible.

  If, after the above exercise, you are still in question about your strengths, you might want to read a book entitled, *Now, Discover Your Strengths*, a self-help book written by Marcus Buckingham and Donald O. Clifton. At the heart of the book is the Internet-based "Clifton Strengths Finder," an online personal assessment that outlines the user's strengths.

> Look for instances and patterns of those 2-3 things that you have done well repeatedly, and that tend to come naturally to you.

- **Start to Explore:** Armed with more conscious knowledge of your natural talents, skills, and passions, begin to research where this combination might gainfully be applied. Your research should include speaking with others and online exploration of various industries and job functions. You will find that this research will begin to narrow your focus. In particular, research those industries and companies that offer strong training or are experiencing or expected to experience strong growth. Where you focus also depends in part on the stage of your career.

■ **Set SMART career objectives**: Identify the roles and growth industries in which you are most interested. Use the SMART methodology for setting near-term, mid-term, and long-term goals regarding the skill sets and experiences that you will need to reach your objectives. SMART is an acronym for:

Specific—pick a specific goal as opposed to something broad or generic

Measurable—choose something you can quantify

Attainable—you should actually be able to attain the career goals you set

Realistic—be objective. For example, it's probably unrealistic to say you'll be a CEO next year, if you're just out of college. A more realistic objective would be to acquire work experiences across multiple functions that are important for a general manager to understand.

Timely—give each goal a timeframe to create a sense of urgency

■ **Monitor your progress**: Put reminders on your calendar with completion dates for specific objectives. If you are not making progress toward your goals, determine why and what you can do to change this. Remember, no one else can do this important work for you.

■ **Identify and seek out "voids"**: Seek internal and external opportunities where there is a pronounced need for you to apply your skill sets. Typically, these are opportunities where your skills fill a distinct void. These "voids" allow you greater opportunity to make an impact, carve out an identity, and build a more powerful and distinct resume. Voids enable you to experience swifter career growth, progress more rapidly, have greater satisfaction, and be paid at a higher level of compensation.

- **Learn to anticipate problems:** Ask yourself, "If this happens, how will I respond?" Develop broader internal relationships at work to better understand others' objectives and potential obstacles to succeeding in your role. Be aware of the objectives, priorities, and activities of your employer's entire company. Don't expect the past to always be an accurate predictor of the future. Stay abreast of the broader dynamics at work within your industry. Without this awareness, it is difficult to anticipate what the future might hold.

- **Own your career**: Importantly, remember that you alone are responsible for the quality of your executive profile and building your track record. Own your performance and hold yourself accountable. Perform by being solutions-focused. Do not get tangled up in "process" beyond what is required. Do not spend time focusing on those things that you cannot control.

> Don't expect the past to always be an accurate predictor of the future.

- **Become a consistent performer**: Career success is not about getting everything right. It is about being consistent and being "right" a lot of the time. It's also about being action-oriented in taking corrective measures when you are not right.

- **Surround yourself with drivers:** Build strong internal relationships with other proactive professionals in your company. Having driven and effective people on your team will make it easier for you to be proactive and succeed. Lazy or incompetent team members will drag you down.

Key Chapter Takeaways:

》 You alone are responsible for the quality of your career. Take control.

》 A proactive mindset will help you shape a more successful career.

》 A game plan created early in your career will shape your success by melding your natural talents, learned skills, and passion in a manner that adds "value," which will be reflected in greater job satisfaction, steadier advancement, and ultimately higher compensation.

Notes:

2

STEP TWO

Cultivate Awareness Skills

"The ultimate value of life depends upon awareness and the power of contemplation rather than upon mere survival." — *Aristotle*

❚❚❚❚

Wikipedia defines "awareness" as the ability to directly know and perceive, to feel, or to be cognizant of events. More broadly, it is the state of being conscious of something. There are multiple types of awareness that will have a profound impact on your career: self-awareness, situational awareness, organizational awareness, feedback awareness, listening awareness and reputation awareness.

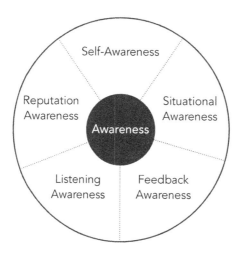

Self-Awareness

The concept of self-awareness is central to career planning and effectiveness as an executive. Self-awareness is defined as "conscious knowledge of one's own character, strengths and weaknesses, feelings, motives and desires." Regardless of your profession or industry, much of your career success rides on your ability to lead, manage, motivate, influence, and build positive relationships with others. Doing this successfully requires well-developed interpersonal skills and emotional intelligence—at the core of which lies self-awareness.

Someone who is self-aware has an accurate understanding of his or her strengths, weaknesses, accomplishments, motivations, values, goals as well as his/her communication style, response to stress and conflict, and personal mission. Aligning self-awareness with your career also creates a higher level of personal satisfaction and success. Similarly, your awareness of the character, feelings and motives of others will provide a foundation for productive interaction with others.

Chances are that if you take time to reflect upon your entire career, you will start to recognize patterns regarding your values, motivations, stress triggers, communication quirks, preferred activities and natural abilities—all of which influence your effectiveness in different professional settings and roles. The most effective and self-aware executives seek out settings and roles where they are able to leverage their core preferences, values and abilities. Less effective executives do not share this same positive alignment, and thus are less fulfilled and successful in their positions.

I remember one particular executive named Frank who was aggressively recruited to a recognized consulting firm. Frank was bright, highly motivated, very credible within his industry, and did outstanding client work. However, his deep-seated drive for personal achievement left an endless stream of broken glass among his coworkers. While Frank was financially very successful and clients valued his work, colleagues did not trust or want to work with him. Despite attempts to coach Frank, his self-awareness—though improved—remained deficient. Ultimately, he was encouraged to leave the firm. He went on to work at another large consulting firm with a similar result. Finally, Frank found a leadership role in a much smaller firm where he did not have to be as concerned about stepping on the toes of his colleagues. He is doing well, but still has a reputation of being tough on subordinates. I anticipate that this shortcoming will create an unhealthy culture in his organization and ultimately make it difficult to attract and keep strong talent. Had Frank gained a sufficient level of self-awareness earlier, and a better understanding of how to team with colleagues, there is no reason why he could not have moved into a leadership role in a larger consulting firm. His hyper-focus on his own achievements was the only thing holding him back.

In another instance, I found myself giving feedback to an accomplished and respected COO of a mid-sized digital company with operations in several regions of the globe. This executive, Mark, had been referred to me for coaching support. Mark had a passionate career objective to become a CEO. After taking sufficient time to get to know Mark and understand his career path, I suggested that it would be useful for me to have some open and candid discussions with his superior (the CEO), his peers and his subordinates to obtain their input. His references indicated that he was commercially successful, operationally effective and a major contributor to his company's success. However, Mark's "soft" skills were in need of development. He'd risen to the C-suite as a result of his operational effectiveness, hard work, persistence, energy, and dedication. He would run through walls, as would his team, to make things happen, and he seldom compromised. These were all admirable executive qualities. However, some saw him as confrontational, overly serious, selfish, tunnel-visioned, focused on his own personal agenda, deliberate, bullish, and hard headed. When confronted directly with this feedback in a summary report that I provided to him, Mark recognized very clearly that he needed to make some changes. He had been somewhat aware of these tendencies previously, but the direct and candid feedback was especially hard-hitting. Mark could have become defensive in receiving this feedback, but instead welcomed it with open arms declaring, "This is gold!"

Because of these shortcomings, Mark's CEO had historically turned to other executives whenever business situations required a high level of sensitivity and an appreciation for the nuances of business relationships. He looked for executives who could influence others directionally without being overly directive. Executives who could create "win-win" solutions when issues arose. These executives accomplished this first by listening with an empathetic ear to understand and entertain another's point of view. They had the ability to analyze the situation and know when it was better to arrive at a workable—as opposed to ideal—solution for the sake of maintaining healthy relationships. Mark realized that to ultimately succeed in a CEO role, he was going to need to develop "soft" skills—entering discussions with an open mind, actively requesting and receiving input from others, being less emotional, and adopting less of a winner-take-all mentality.

Through the subsequent coaching, Mark is becoming less territorial and recognizing how strong solutions can be formed with collective input from others. He is learning to be more tolerant of those who have opposing points of view. He is demonstrating that he wants to be more open to change, and less a creature of habit. Importantly, he is becoming more nuanced in his communications and less emotional. These changes are not easy, but Mark is strongly motivated by the recognition that these changes are an opportunity to become even more effective as a leader. We have developed a straight forward behavior modification program whereby Mark focuses on one key area of change each day of the week, week after week, until the five selected behavioral changes become habit. He keeps a list of these five behavioral changes on a half slip of paper at the office, at home, and in his wallet. What's more, he keeps a pebble in his pants pocket as a reminder to focus on the noted behavioral change each day. Every time he puts his hand in his pocket, he feels the pebble and focuses on the required behavioral change.

Situational Awareness

Situational awareness is critical for business leaders and managers. Ignoring facts or blindly pursuing goals may end with disastrous consequences. What is situational awareness in a business context? It is the ability of a business manager to:

- Observe what is going on around him or her (within the economy, an industry, marketplace, or company)
- Properly frame what is occurring and why
- Assess potential corresponding threats to the business
- Decide on a course of action
- Carry out that action

Situational awareness empowers professionals to anticipate needed actions, be alert to potential challenges, and understand where an organization's focus needs to be at any given moment. Situational awareness is developed through experience and training. It grows with your exposure to different situations and your ability to gather and rapidly assimilate information. In order to develop situational awareness, it is helpful to seek out experiences in different roles and a range of industries. Experience managing through full economic cycles also heightens an executive's situational awareness and ability to respond rapidly to similar conditions in the future.

Different business conditions (i.e., situations) exhibit distinct patterns that aware and experienced executives recognize and react to. For example, executives accustomed to operating in high-growth environments are attuned to the importance of ensuring continued levels of high product and service quality. An executive who has experienced multiple turnarounds develops a situational awareness for the key operational levers needed to facilitate profit improvement while taking actions to revitalize revenue growth. Startups have their own unique situational challenges and opportunities. Professionals involved with startups must be fully attuned to available funding and cash burn as they build internal resources. They have an awareness of how specific actions will impact the value and growth potential of the company. Individuals with a high degree of situational awareness have an innate "feel" for such situations, people, and events as they play out. They know the variables that the executive or manager can control, and which ones they cannot.

> Individuals with a high degree of situational awareness have an innate "feel" for such situations, people, and events as they play out.

Private equity firms learned many years ago that the difference between a successful and mediocre investment very often comes down to the experience and situational awareness of the CEO in the portfolio company. Specifically, the ability of the CEO to rapidly assess a business and industry, react by making critical decisions, and aggressively drive proper actions. This is why in many CEO searches for private equity firm portfolio companies the position requirements are more focused on relevant industry and "situation" experience—i.e., growth or turnaround, or acquisition and roll-up experience.

Organizational Awareness

Individuals with high organizational awareness keep abreast of what is occurring in other parts of the company which could impact their own actions and thinking and the people they manage and lead. An organizationally aware executive understands the broader goals and objectives of the company and how he or she fits into the bigger puzzle. He or she has an appreciation for where and how decisions are made, the objectives and motives of other departments, and which colleagues can be counted on for their support. Organizationally aware executives assimilate, organize, and interpret formal and informal information streams on a daily basis.

How do you become more organizationally aware? You listen, observe, and get out of your office. You take an active interest in what colleagues are doing. You put yourself into situations where you can observe a variety of input. Cross-functional committees and task forces are an ideal venue for doing this. Unfortunately, many business professionals become so busy with day-to-day activities, overbooked schedules, and achieving near-term goals that they do not take sufficient time to routinely engage sufficiently with other parts of the organization.

If you are by nature a highly focused individual who becomes deeply absorbed in projects, tuning out all else that is happening around you, the odds are great that you do not have well-developed organizational awareness. This lack of organizational awareness impedes not only your personal performance but the performance of those you manage. This becomes visible through ineffective plans that are created in a vacuum, programs that are not properly pre-sold to the organization, and less enthusiastic backup of support functions when objectives are misaligned. In my experience, executives with high levels of situational awareness do not seclude themselves, but rather engage readily and broadly with others in the company and their industry.

I recently coached a senior data science leader, Jon, who works in a healthcare insurance company. Jon was a very bright, competent and uniquely qualified professional in his arena—an M.D. with an actuarial undergraduate degree plus a top tier MBA. He was passionate about his work—delivering quality patient care, fairly priced, and in a cost-effective manner. Jon tended to be somewhat introverted, preferred to see things in black and white, and struggled in dealing with ambiguity. This is not uncommon with data science professionals. More importantly, he did not actively get out of his office to engage with the broader organization. His understanding of the broader organizational structure—who's who and spheres of influence—was not well developed. He was highly respected by his team of fifty professionals who he worked with closely. However, he did not proactively engage at the same level with his peers and superior. Not surprisingly, his peers and superior, while they thought well of him, did not rate his performance as highly as his subordinates had.

Jon and I are presently working on getting him out of his office and relying more on face-to-face and phone communications with others in the firm instead of primarily email correspondence. He is also working on being more visible with his and his team's achievements by directly engaging internal clients. He is doing this by inviting them to appropriate meetings and issuing progress reports to keep them abreast of activity. Finally, Jon is beginning to explore where there is opportunity to become more broadly involved in activities across the business.

A further example of the benefits of broader involvement occurred with another manager I know in a separate company. He petitioned for inclusion in a multi-departmental task force, wanting to gain greater visibility across the organization. He shortly realized a further benefit in being part of this task force—that of being exposed to input and news from across the organization. As a result of this added perspective, he was able to synchronize his business plans and actions with the rapidly evolving priorities of the company.

Feedback Awareness

Executives who openly seek formal and informal feedback throughout the course of their careers achieve more rapid personal growth. Formal feedback consists of annual or periodic performance reviews as well as input from mentors and coaches. Informal feedback consists of the signals that you receive from others throughout the course of your daily activities—meetings, presentations, teleconferences, customer interface, and one-on-one discussions. Recognizing, receiving and acting on this formal and informal feedback results in higher levels of self-awareness and an ability to engage more effectively with others. This ability to engage more effectively with superiors, peers, and subordinates promotes greater trust, openness, and sharing of information. Ultimately, this leads to higher situational awareness, resulting in better and timelier business decisions. These decisions have a direct and positive impact on your career.

You can develop greater feedback awareness through focused observation of verbal and non-verbal (body language) cues. This takes practice but can be accomplished if you engage openly and listen intently to others. Oftentimes, this means setting aside your own agenda, and acknowledging and considering the merit of external input. The more you hear opposing points of view from others, the more you need to consider their input—not ignore it.

One of my initial search assignments with Spencer Stuart involved two well-qualified candidates who were not selected for the executive position that I was charged with filling. The assignment was for Vice President of Marketing with a Chicago-based consumer package goods manufacturer. Both of the two runners-up for the role asked me why they had not been chosen. Eager to enrich the professional growth of these executives, I set aside time with each candidate to provide direct, constructive feedback.

I told the first candidate—who was exceptionally capable—that he was not selected for the position because he had come across as a "know it all" and did not appear to have the required listening skills for the position. This, I told him, led to uncertainty about his ability to collaborate with others, a requirement for the job. The unfortunate aspect about this feedback is that I had noted this tendency when I initially assessed him for the client. At that time, I strongly encouraged him to have a more balanced conversation with the client—to do more listening and have an interactive dialogue. I explained to him that interactive dialogues allow for better chemistry to develop. In my experience, candidates appreciate honest input and feedback if provided in a manner that is intended to help them. Unfortunately, in this instance the candidate did not fully hear or consider the input that I provided.

I explained to the second candidate—who was less senior than the first candidate, but still well qualified for the position—that he had shown up at the client's offices looking rumpled and a bit disheveled, despite my earlier coaching. This had not impressed the interviewer. Additionally, I explained, he had less experience in developing larger teams. In this case, my feedback was received and appreciated. This candidate recognized that his profile was still a "work in process."

Years later, I had occasion to run into both individuals at our firm's annual Marketing Officer Summit in New York. The first candidate still had a tendency to be in transmit versus receiving mode when communicating, and I learned that his career had stalled.

The second candidate—once rumpled—was now well-groomed and dressed. His demeanor and diction had become crisper, inspiring a stronger level of confidence. He remarked how the feedback I'd provided years earlier had encouraged him to continue to seek out and be open to input from others. In fact, as a result of my feedback, he had sought out team-building assignments in order to acquire the skills he was missing in his professional profile. Furthermore, he made a point to seek and select opportunities to work with individuals willing to provide constructive feedback on a regular basis. Importantly, his growth was made possible due to his openness to the feedback he received. As a result of his willingness to act upon the feedback he received, this professional's career had continued to move forward.

Listening Awareness

Great listening skills are not only critical for receiving and acting on feedback, but also play a profound role in your ability to lead, manage and influence others. During your next conversations with others, take note of whether you are focused on listening. Are you available, interested, and open to hearing what the other person is saying? Or, are you more concerned with pressing your agenda, showing how much you know, or controlling the conversation? As we so clearly saw in the preceding example of the stalled executive, his lack of listening skills impeded his career advancement. If you have never taken the time to record your phone discussions at the office, do so (with permission, of course). Listening to yourself and others in these interchanges can be very instructive.

Effective listening skills are an absolute requirement for engaging, communicating and building productive relationships. The more senior you are in an organization, the more important listening awareness becomes. Why? As you advance in your career, you will increasingly rely on others for support and to get things done. This is the essence of leadership. Without listening awareness, you become isolated and, at worst, ill informed. Listening awareness will become a key determinant of your career success. If you are an active listener, others will want to engage and team with you, and your accomplishments will be richer.

Reputation Awareness

The quality of your reputation has a direct impact on the array of job opportunities that are presented to you, the strength of your candidacy for a new position, the quality of talent you are able to attract to your team, how others treat you, and ultimately the level of success that you achieve in your career. Your reputation is the sum of many parts—your interactions with others, the internal and external perception of the quality of your work, the results you achieve, your grit and resilience, the integrity you exhibit in your professional and personal lives, your recognized work ethic and ability to dig into the weeds when necessary. Like self-awareness, reputation awareness requires you to become aware of your impact on your company and your coworkers. If you feel that aspects of your reputation are undeveloped or unwarranted, it's your responsibility to improve them.

Your reputation becomes either stronger or weaker with every phone conversation, every presentation, every interaction, and every decision you make whether professional or personal. How many times have we heard of someone's personal life casting a shadow on their professional standing? The harsh truth about reputations is that they take a lot of time, effort and energy to build. However, they can be severely tarnished or implode overnight—irreparably harmed over a single incident or lack of judgement, especially in today's viral world of social media. Yet, everybody has bad days and we all make mistakes. Strive for excellence. When you fail, take ownership, learn from your mistakes and strive to do better thereafter. The real problem is not the occasional misstep that we all experience. Rather, it's when a destructive mindset takes over. Don't let power and success go to your head. Don't be greedy. Remain humble even as your title and responsibilities grow. Share the credit. Continue to empower and support others.

> The harsh truth about reputations is that they take a lot of time, effort and energy to build.

A number of years ago, I conducted a challenging search for a Chief Commercial Officer who would be the number two executive in a $180 million privately held manufacturer of electronic Point of Service (POS) systems for retailers and gas stations. The challenge with the search was that the company was located in a small Midwestern town. After considerable effort, we found and presented a candidate our client liked. He was an exceptional fit from both an experience and personality perspective. As we began to formulate an offer, conduct final references, and verify education…a snag developed. We were unable to verify the candidate's undergraduate degree.

When confronted with this issue, the candidate had no explanation as to why the school did not have a record. Several days went by and we were still unable to confirm his education. Finally, the candidate called me to explain that he had never received his full degree. I asked why his resume showed a full degree and his graduation year. He replied that he had misled us. I explained to him that his broader integrity and reputation now came into question and that he had put us in a very difficult spot with our client. I shared this unwelcome information with our client who made the decision not to go forward with the job offer. Our client commented, "I'm much less concerned about whether a well-qualified executive has a full college degree. But, the fact that he misled us is a disqualifier. How could I ever trust him with my business?" Because of a lack of integrity, and perhaps his own insecurity, this well-qualified candidate lost out on a terrific opportunity and destroyed his reputation with our firm. While our client was extremely disappointed with the turn of events, he appreciated our integrity in coming forward immediately with this finding. It never crossed our minds to do otherwise.

Developing Awareness

It's clear that mastering multiple types of awareness is central to your career success. Like having a proactive mindset, mastering awareness requires conscious and focused observation and active consideration for what has been observed. If you cannot consider the meaning and impact of these observations in the moment, than do so later. Only then are you in a position to determine what needs to be done and how high a priority it should be. Below, I offer some suggestions to get you started.

- Practice mindfulness. Mindfulness is the ability to be present in the moment—undistracted and focused on what is going on around you. Mindfulness enables you to make keener observations.

- Set aside ten minutes at the end of each day to mentally take note of your observations and important pieces of input you received throughout your day.

- Reflect on both positive and not so positive observations and input, what these mean to you, and where your thinking and behavior are well aligned or need to be modified. This reflection creates consciousness and sets the stage for determining how you can change your thinking and behavior, if needed.

■ Periodically, share your observations and input with trusted colleagues to check the validity of your observations.

Key Chapter Takeaways

)) Awareness is an ability that we all have in varying degrees. It can be practiced and further developed.

)) Higher levels of awareness result in stronger relationship building, communications, influencing, decision making and job performance.

)) Professionals who aspire to executive-level leadership must seek out opportunities to develop their key areas of awareness: self-awareness, situational awareness, organizational awareness, feedback awareness, listening awareness and reputation awareness.

)) Professionals with limited awareness who are not open to professional feedback will stall in their careers.

)) Professionals with higher levels of awareness do a better job of managing their careers and aligning their skills and interests with specific functions and industry sectors.

Notes:

3

STEP THREE

Optimize Your Market Positioning

"If all you're trying to do is essentially the same thing as your rivals, then it's unlikely that you'll be very successful." — *Michael Porter*

Do you ever think about your professional profile relative to the supply and demand for talent in the job market? Have you considered how many people there are with profiles similar to your own? Do you have an informed appreciation for how much market demand there is for executives with your experience and skill sets? If you answered "yes" to these three questions, you are aware of your broader positioning in the market. This understanding enables you to make strategic and positive career development decisions. Taken together, these decisions and corresponding actions determine your market value. If you did not answer the three questions affirmatively, a deliberate application of basic supply-and-demand market principles throughout your career will pay large dividends. How you choose to develop, position, and differentiate yourself in the marketplace makes a definite impact on your career progression, job satisfaction, and long-term compensation.

Let's dig deeper into four different supply-and-demand talent scenarios to demonstrate the impact that positioning can have on your career:

- High Market Demand / Limited Talent Supply
- Low Market Demand / High Talent Supply
- High Market Demand / High Talent Supply
- Low Market Demand / Low Talent Supply

Your positioning in one of these quadrants has a direct impact on:

- The number of professionals you will compete against for a given position
- The number and quality of opportunities with which you will be presented
- The amount of compensation leverage you will be able to exert
- The rate at which you'll be able to advance your career

High Demand/Limited Supply

If your professional profile is positioned in this quadrant of the marketplace, you are absolutely golden! You are not only one of a limited number of executives who do what you do, but organizations are fiercely competing to get your attention. You have done a masterful job (or are very lucky) in thoughtfully positioning your skill sets and profile in a function and/or industry sector that has high or growing demand and a limited supply of professionals who meet the job requirements.

As a result, you have benefited from the simple laws of supply and demand in two ways:

1. You have multiple job opportunities from which to select
2. You enjoy a higher level of compensation

Opportunities in this quadrant of the market are often found in emerging industries and emerging job functions. If you are observant of such industry trends and jump in early, the benefits can be tremendous. This was certainly true for those executives who first sensed that the Internet would have a major impact on how people communicated, accessed and shared information as well as purchased goods and services. In 1997, professionals with the skills to service this growing sector essentially did not exist. However, professionals with core foundational skills who were paying attention to this trend sought opportunities to learn new skills and be in the vanguard of this momentous change. Many of these professionals recognized the development of a large, emerging future talent void, and had the courage and foresight to take advantage of it. Others stumbled across it because of their curiosity. There were still others in senior roles, also observant, who did not have the career flexibility or timing to personally dive in head-first. Instead, they hired early Internet talent for their organizations and worked closely with technology providers and digital ad agencies to develop their knowledgebase and organization's capabilities. Developing this early understanding and mindset allowed them to position themselves for future leadership opportunities, many of which were unimagined at the time. Today, many of these individuals—especially the early adopters—are heads of ecommerce and multichannel businesses across a variety of industry sectors. Others with this understanding were able to jump to pure-play Internet companies where their more traditional management backgrounds, skill sets, and maturity were valued.

A more current example of a role in the High Demand/Low Supply quadrant is the growing need for Chief Information Security Officers and cybersecurity specialists. The increasing incidence of cyberattacks through ransomware, advanced phishing ploys, and critical data hacks pose a grave threat to the misuse of sensitive or personal information and privacy for consumers, corporations, and government institutions. In the May 16, 2017 issue of *The Wall Street Journal,* an article entitled, "Demand Jumps for Cybersecurity Experts," noted such talent is in short supply with unfilled jobs expected to number 1.8 million in 2022, up 20% from 2015. "Only 65% of today's firms have a Chief Information

Security Officer. The role demands a cool head, strong interpersonal skills, and great technical savvy."

Opportunities like this abound, primarily due to the continued pace of innovation and technology advancements. Innovation and technology, as we have clearly witnessed across multiple industry sectors, disrupts and threatens traditional business models. Successful companies either lead through innovation, or aggressively respond to this disruption. These dynamics create ongoing demand for talented professionals who evolve their skill sets and experience to fill talent voids. If you are observant of emerging technologies and reflect on how they impact or disrupt markets, you will develop a perspective on where emerging job opportunities can be found. To develop this awareness, read broadly, talk with others outside your normal circle of contacts, and attend industry conferences that you would not previously have considered attending. This will help you connect the dots.

> Successful companies either lead through innovation, or aggressively respond to this disruption.

We live in exciting times, ripe with opportunities to shape your career. The Internet and digital technology, social media and online marketplaces will continue to shape industry sectors for years to come. Think about the potential impact of technologies such as augmented and Virtual Reality, artificial intelligence, the Internet of Things, driverless cars, nanosensors, next generation batteries, and 3-D printing. How will these technologies impact your industry and create new job opportunities for you?

Low Demand/High Supply

In the Low Demand/High Supply quadrant of the talent market, many people have similar profiles and there are fewer jobs to go around. This is the most challenging quadrant to be positioned in. Finding yourself in this quadrant can be the result of industry consolidation, outsourcing of capabilities to less costly labor markets, economic cycles and situations where once sought-after skills have become obsolete due to advances in technology. In yet other instances, the supply of talent for specific roles simply catches up with demand.

Examples of Low Demand/High Supply scenarios resulting from disruption, industry decline and consolidation and outsourcing include manufacturing, traditional publishing, retail, and for-profit education, to name a few. This dynamic can also occur in cyclical sectors such as the oil and gas industry and financial services.

One current and acute example of a Low Demand/High Supply scenario is occurring in the stock brokerage industry. This industry has experienced the perfect storm, consisting of disintermediation brought about by online discount brokerages, declining revenue, industry consolidation and heightened government regulation. Add to these pressures, the negative impact of index funds, "robo-advisors" and an increase in passive investing…and the future looks challenging for all but the largest or most agile brokerage firms.

If you find yourself in the Low Demand/High Supply quadrant, your professional profile is not meaningfully differentiated. This challenge has the potential to lead to a positive outcome if you adapt and learn new skills and prepare to reposition yourself in a different, growing industry. If you have not taken these actions, you will find yourself positioned among the masses in a low growth sector. If the latter is the case, the simple laws of supply and demand will continue to diminish the value of your professional profile and significantly reduce your leverage to negotiate higher compensation.

If you find yourself in any of these scenarios, you may well be concerned about keeping the job that you have. This is not a very pleasant way to exist. It's never too late to make a change, but it will take an immediate and concerted effort. You will need to consider more robust industry sectors where there is greater demand for your experience and skills and the supply of talented professionals is more limited. This might require making a lateral move in compensation and job title in the short run while you learn and gain skills and credibility in the new sector. In the long run, this short-term sacrifice has a greater likelihood of leading to long-term security and advancement.

If you have not previously had the experience of transitioning into a new industry sector, you will want to be especially mindful about the move. You want to identify sectors that are in a growth mode and that have demand for your skill sets. Additionally, the new sector should have enough similarities in the business model to your prior industry that a portion of your experience and knowledge base can be leveraged. This increases the likelihood of a successful transition. Until you have developed transition skills across several sectors, stay closer in to your prior experience.

High Demand/High Supply

If the High Demand / High Supply quadrant is where you are positioned, all is not lost. You have the potential to thoughtfully reposition or enhance your profile to distinguish yourself from your peers. Identify what is distinct about your background and can be further leveraged, or decide what additional experiences and skill sets will help to differentiate you within your industry. You may also want to consider leveraging your experience and skill sets into a new industry sector that is growing and has a smaller pool of talented professionals, as we discussed above. We will further discuss industry transitions later in the book.

The accounting industry is an example of a sector with high demand and high supply. There are roughly 660,000 Certified Public Accountants in the U.S. and 1,300,000 accountants and auditors. Such significant numbers mean that while demand may be strong, if you stumble or underperform, there are many others who can step into your shoes—that is, unless you have distinguished or differentiated your profile in some way. Other large, well-established service industries share this dynamic—for example, advertising, law and even executive search.

Over the years, executive search—my former profession—has undergone substantial change. When I began my search career in the mid-80s, consultants tended to be generalists working across industries and job functions. As the search market matured and clients became more demanding, the industry developed specialist consultants for specific industry sectors and job functions. Search firms now have individual consultants who specialize in legal searches, CFO searches, CIO, supply chain, marketing, communications, CEO and board director assignments. Similarly, we have industry specialists with expertise in financial services assignments, non-profits, health care, pharmaceutical, retail, digital transformation, travel and hospitality, technology, telecommunications, media, consumer durables, manufacturing, energy, and professional services. Consultants and search firms who continued to function as generalists versus building recognized specialty practices with deep domain knowledge ultimately were unable to compete and left the market. Below, I share a very personal example of what I did to reposition myself in the search industry.

I was fortunate to join what became the top firm in our industry, Spencer Stuart. The brand equity of Spencer Stuart and the firm's reputation for doing high quality work at the top end of the market was a differentiator I benefited from. I started as a generalist search consultant with a consumer marketing bent, based on my background in consumer goods and services. Being one of the two youngest consultants in this global firm at the time I joined, I spent my early years conducting highly challenging searches across a broad array of industries and job functions with companies headquartered in less attractive geographies. These were often the assignments others did not want to conduct. While painful at the time, in retrospect, this proved to be beneficial for my development and

> While painful at the time, in retrospect, this proved to be beneficial for my development and breadth of perspective.

breadth of perspective. I also conducted substantial work for consumer package goods companies. However, these felt more like "cookie cutter" assignments and did not hold my interest.

Recognizing that "specialization" was the future of the industry, I began to think strategically about trends in the consumer markets and how I might position and differentiate myself within the firm and industry. At this time, computers, data, targeted marketing and targeted business models were experiencing strong growth. Direct marketing as an industry and job market was not being particularly well served by the search industry at the top management level. I developed a proposal and funding request to build a Direct Marketing Practice for Spencer Stuart, which was approved. The proposal was positioned to further differentiate our Consumer Goods and Services Practice. In the ensuing years, we built the leading Direct Marketing Practice in the industry, conducting the most senior level work for recognized catalog companies, credit card providers, insurance companies, and membership service firms, among others. We became so well respected that our firm was selected to conduct a very high visibility CEO search for the Direct Marketing Association, whose Board of Directors included leading industry CEOs.

> Direct marketing as an industry and job market was not being particularly well served by the search industry.

Then, around 1996, I started to read increasingly about something called the Internet. The projected growth curves around this technology were staggering. Given my familiarity with direct-to-consumer business models, it became apparent to me that the Internet would rapidly become "direct marketing on steroids." Even better, Internet executive talent was not readily available in the market and many companies would have executive search needs. I could hardly contain my excitement as I developed a proposal to morph the Direct Marketing Practice into the Direct

Marketing & E-Commerce Practice. When the first substantial E-Christmas occurred in 1998, we were well positioned to ride the wave. In the ensuing five years, almost every major retailer in the country needed E-Commerce leadership. With the help of colleagues, we developed powerful intellectual capital about the leadership and talent needs required for the emerging Internet economy. These studies generated client awareness and interest in our capabilities across multiple industry sectors. We developed a special forum—the Digital Leadership Exchange (DLX)—for digital, ecommerce and Internet top executives to get to know each other. We later brought in Google to co-sponsor and co-brand these events, further supporting our leadership position in the sector. We expanded DLX globally and used it as a venue for engaging Spencer Stuart colleagues around the globe with Internet leaders in their local markets. Along the way, the Direct & E-Commerce Practice morphed once again into our Internet Practice, and yet again into our Digital Transformation Practice. Many colleagues took part in growing the Practice. What an exciting and rewarding eighteen years it was!

Our proactive approach to innovation and market positioning paid off handsomely at Spencer Stuart. The same can happen for your career. Such opportunities are all around us. You simply have to develop the habit of looking for them. For example, another talent market likely to be reshaped in the near future is the legal profession. The digitization of legal documents, cases and information combined with the capabilities of artificial intelligence (i.e., natural language processing) and sophisticated search engines will require fewer newly minted legal associates for conducting research. Already much of this type of work (electronic discovery, due diligence, and contract review) is being conducted through artificial intelligence. This technology is

> Such opportunities are all around us. You simply have to develop the habit of looking for them.

anticipated to result in the unbundling and outsourcing of such legal services. More than 280 legal technology startups have raised $757 million since 2012.

Should you be positioned in the High Demand/High Supply quadrant, you have three potential courses of action to competitively reposition yourself:

- Enhance your profile with value-added experiences, understanding or skill sets that others do not broadly possess. For example, if you are a traditional marketing executive, you could develop an understanding of how to apply artificial intelligence to generate a superior return on marketing dollars spent.

- Identify growth opportunities in a sector or company where your skill sets and experience are transferrable. One executive I know—a classically trained brand marketer—joined eBay in its early years and expanded the brand and service into Europe and beyond.

- Become increasingly specialized in an arena that is underserved, much like my journey at Spencer Stuart.

Low Demand/Low Supply

Professionals in the Low Demand/Low Supply quadrant are often those who have highly specialized interests and skills and tend to carve out unique professional niches. These individuals are often driven more by their personal passion and mission than compensation, title or power. Positions in this quadrant reflect intellectual or creative pursuits more than broad practical skill sets. Examples in this quadrant can include highly specialized roles in areas such as scientific research, legal services, asset valuation, education policy formulation, complex financial derivatives, and econometrics.

Candidates in low demand and low supply professions generally have moderate levels of compensation unless they have developed broadly respected reputations in their field. This is a reflection of the narrow markets that they often serve. If you operate in this quadrant of the market and are at all concerned about your long-term viability, you may want to consider repositioning your skills to serve other markets or try supplementing your background with more practical training. Networking with others in your field and understanding how their careers have taken shape can provide useful context. There's definitely not a "one size fits all" template for a career in the Low Demand/Low Supply quadrant.

Build and Strengthen Your Market Position

Have you identified which quadrant your profile fits into? Throughout your career, you should consistently seek ways to enhance your positioning relative to the demand for talent and perceived supply of capable professionals in your quadrant. Towards this end, you will want to build skill sets in a manner that will meaningfully distinguish you from the masses. The most successful executives I know have an understanding of how to consciously shape and position their experience and talents to fill significant existing or emerging talent "voids" in an industry or company.

When commencing your career, you may choose to start with a well-recognized, large organization for training and learning purposes. This will help you build foundational skill sets and disciplines. In this case, you will likely find that your entering "class" consists of 15 to 40 or more peers with backgrounds similar to your own. You will be one of many doing pretty much the same thing. If you stumble, there will be someone ready to fill your shoes. Until you distinguish yourself from this peer group—either through exemplary performance or by developing some unique and needed skill sets—your career advancement will likely be at a measured pace.

Another early career option is to join a mid-sized organization with a positive reputation but somewhat less structure and hierarchy than a larger entity. In this scenario, you will likely have less depth of formal training. However, you also have fewer peer competitors, more interaction with managers several levels above you, and wider latitude for contributing to the success of the organization. The skills that you bring into the organization, or develop while there, will be less duplicative. These environments make it possible for you to gain additional responsibilities rapidly. Additionally, these scenarios often provide more opportunity to appreciate the entirety of the organization's operations and gain exposure across a broader array of business functions. You will want to weigh the tradeoffs between a larger versus smaller company and determine which scenario is more comfortable for you and suitable for your goals.

¶ ¶ ¶ ¶

Robert is a real-life case study that illustrates the benefits of a smaller, mid-sized organization. As a young executive, he joined a growing $500 million (mid-sized) provider of airline Wi-Fi services. His background in data structures and algorithms, machine learning, and mathematical modeling was well suited for the job. Very quickly it became apparent to Robert that the company had a treasure trove of pricing and usage data around individual flight segments. This "big data," as it is known, was being underutilized. If properly structured, Robert believed this data could provide the company with valuable business insights. He took the initiative to import new software capabilities from outside the organization to analyze the performance of numerous price tests and merchandising initiatives, which he then shared with his superior. Shortly thereafter, he was provided the opportunity to present his findings to senior and top management at the company. In his presentation, Robert employed easy-to-read graphical visualizations of large data sets to exhibit the results of the advanced analyses and communicate key findings and business opportunities. Since this presentation, Robert has been given the opportunity to create tools for automated reporting of key business metrics and product performance. He has also partnered with the company's sales teams to generate pricing and usage models for both targeted and large-scale commercial airline partnerships. Additionally, he has taken the initiative to organize and teach an 8-week course on these new capabilities. Most importantly, he has generated incremental growth in subscriber revenue.

Today, Robert's skills, knowledge, and inquisitive/creative mind are uniquely positioned within this mid-sized company. He has been promoted twice in the last two years and now oversees revenue management for the company. This level of responsibility, latitude for creative thinking, and exposure to senior and top management would have been less available to Robert in a larger and more structured corporation.

▪ ▪ ▪ ▪

What can you learn from Robert's experience that will help you distinguish your professional profile and customize your own supply-and-demand curve?

- Robert's proactive identification of untapped data and analytics opportunities and the resulting business buildings insights provided him visibility and credibility with senior management. This resulted in additional assignments and funding, allowing him to build additional skill sets and accomplish more goals. This separated him from his peers and led to promotions and increased responsibility. Follow Robert's example and seek out opportunities that will help you add valuable dimensions to your profile and begin to create your unique storyline in the company and market.

- Seek out challenges, fill "voids," and add value.

- Take on projects that others shy away from.

- Position your profile, ideally, in a growth industry, or a growth role. A growth role is one that can leverage aspects of your background in a position or function of increasing importance.

- As you progress in your career, develop a well-informed perspective on where the growth-oriented opportunities are or are likely to develop. It is a lot easier to exhibit successes and add value in a growth scenario than in a mature or contracting industry or organization. It also tends to be more satisfying and result in building a stronger resume.

Identifying future career opportunities requires an understanding of current developments in your industry and related sectors. Maintaining an active reading list of professional and industry publications and selectively attending national and global conferences will provide you with insights on emerging growth opportunities. It will also help you anticipate emerging supply-and-demand dynamics.

If you are involved in the communications, media or technology sectors, for example, you should probably understand the impact of mobile technology and the significance of 5G (fifth generation wireless). By attending conferences and taking the time for related reading, you can develop an understanding of how these technologies might impact your company, position and industry. You will gain insight into evolving requirements of leaders in your field. You can also begin to understand where future growth opportunities lie and where you can opportunistically position or supplement your experience. You may want to actively consider areas as diverse as cybersecurity, the Internet of Things, artificial intelligence, new developments in content, data, and advertising. A curious mind is a tremendous professional asset, especially in sectors that change rapidly. A curious mind, agility and adaptability are antidotes to becoming obsolete.

Consider an Industry Transition

Moving from one industry to another, if done successfully, is another way to strengthen your market position. Successfully navigating an industry transition signals to others that you are able to take your skills across sectors. Industry transitions can provide you with renewed intellectual stimulation and help you reposition your talents in an industry or organization that presents stronger growth potential.

In the process of transitioning successfully, you demonstrate your ability to observe, learn, adapt, and be impactful in new settings. Having done so once, employers and recruiters are more likely to believe you can do it again in other businesses and sectors. This additional breadth of experience opens up an array of potential opportunities. What you can accomplish through a successful industry transition is a permanent improvement of your position on the supply-and-demand curve.

> This additional breadth of experience opens up an array of potential opportunities.

Why do organizations look outside their industry? Oftentimes, an organization's executive team believes that the best talent solutions can be found in other industry sectors. They may require skills that cannot be found within their own industry. Perhaps a company's management team believes they are the best at what they do and their competitors' talent is inferior. In this case, they look to other sectors where talent for a specific function is stronger or the talent universe deeper. There are also a few companies that are so unique they do not have competitors and must therefore look in other sectors for all their talent.

We will further discuss successful industry transitions later in the book when we take a look at the ten building blocks of successful career management.

Develop Leadership Skills

Developing your leadership skills and reputation is a critical component of enhancing your market positioning. Companies are thirsting for leaders. Much of my past thirty years at Spencer Stuart was devoted to recognizing and assessing leadership potential. While *The Proactive Executive* is not a book about leadership, I would be remiss if I did not provide some insight on leadership as it relates to career advancement.

al definition of leadership is as follows: "The ability
ial to chart a course, build a talented team and followers, and produce desirable outcomes for the purpose of achieving a mission or project of significance." Charting a course often
involves an element of thought leadership as well as a vision for
reaching a destination that has a positive influence on the goals
of an organization. Leadership can be exhibited at any level of an
organization. The effectiveness of leadership is measured by results
achieved, the ability to build high-performing and motivated
teams and create positive and effective cultures. Executive profiles of leaders are like snowflakes—no two are alike. Leadership
requirements for a large and complex multinational company are
vastly different than those for a startup. The executive leadership
profile for one industry sector will likely be quite different from
the ideal leadership profile in another. The profile of a banking
leader is vastly different than that of a top manufacturing executive. In each setting, the effective leader possesses both sufficient
cognitive and interpersonal skills as well as relevant experience.

The best leaders I've known have the following attributes:

- Uncommon intelligence or learning agility
- Sufficient to high level of self-awareness
- Ability to get the right things done
- Organizational and situational smarts
- Foundational skills, technical competence and experience
- Passion and unwavering focus on mission and purpose
- High energy, grit and resilience
- A positive, confident attitude
- Strong analytical and strategic skills
- Ability to build great teams
- Willingness to take calculated risks
- Well-developed communication and presentation skills

- Ability to influence and inspire confidence in others

- A take-charge attitude, willingness to shoulder accountability

- Vision for the future

- Sociability and charisma

- Decisiveness

- Great judgment and integrity

- Strength in uncertain times

- Stability amid the pressures and vagaries of business

Are leaders born or made? Based on my experience assessing literally thousands of senior executives during my career with Spencer Stuart, I strongly believe that a small percentage of executives are what we refer to as natural "born" leaders. In my view, leadership is the result of both nature and nurture. More specifically, I consider leadership to be the result of having a sufficient level of innate qualities that we are born with—brain, body, and temperament traits, which account for roughly one-third of the leadership equation—and accumulating the right experiences, education, and training, which accounts for roughly two-thirds of the leadership equation. Of these three components (experience, education, and training), experience and training are more important.

> In my view, leadership is the result of both nature and nurture.

Overall, this is great news for the large percentage of us who are not born leaders. To become a leader, you will want to develop fundamental skills and abilities related to critical thinking, effective communication, influencing, relationship building, and cultivating greater awareness as we have previously discussed. Seek and embrace new challenges and increasingly complex learning experiences that will facilitate the acquisition of these fundamental skills and abilities. Understand the career paths of respected leaders in your company and industry. Knowing how they rose to their current roles will inform your own career planning. Observe the current leaders in your organization and what they do, and how they do it. Enroll in leadership development programs. Read broadly about leadership principles and practices and determine where you can apply these in your daily activity. Doing these things and continuing to perform at a high level will put you on the right path to becoming a leader. With experience, you will develop your own formula for successful leadership.

While conducting interviews with a range of executives for this book, I had the distinct pleasure of sitting with Walter "Wally" D. Scott. For many years, Wally taught a very popular course on leadership at Northwestern University's Kellogg Business School. Prior to teaching at Kellogg, Wally held a series of leadership roles, including: Senior Managing Director of Lehman Brothers, EVP and Chief Financial Officer of Pillsbury Company, CEO and then Chairman of an American Express subsidiary, and Chairman of Grand Metropolitan, Inc. He was kind enough to share the following formula for successful leadership, which I pass on to you here:

- Select exceptional people and commit to helping them succeed. Support them and create an environment that unleashes their discretionary efforts, remembering that each person is unique and special.

- Leadership is about trust—earn it…and integrity—live it. Character matters.

- Live the behaviors you wish others to adopt, and be sure that there is nothing that you ask of others that you would not do yourself.

- Make your values visible by modeling what is important and what you honor. Be authentic. Followers will ask, "Is this leader real and will he or she always do what he or she says?"

- Be an exceptional follower. Do everything in your power to help your leader succeed.

- Communicate effectively. Listen and observe first and, most importantly, listen for what is not said.

- Listen to the small voices inside you. Intuition and experience matter. Balance analysis and logic with judgment and wisdom.

- Encourage fresh viewpoints and dissent. Protect and honor differing perspectives. Keep reinventing your organization and challenging the status quo. It and you can be better.

- Cultivate diverse and challenging sources of information within and outside your organization.

- Reach for opportunities which stretch and challenge you, so that you continue to grow. Keep reinventing yourself.

- Set high standards for yourself. Outperform the expectations of others as well as the demands of the job.

- Be sure your leadership and all other aspects of the organization are playing the same music—that your actions and words communicate a consistent message that is lived throughout the enterprise.

- Be passionate. Have commitment. They are necessary to lift an organization and an individual to the greatest heights.

- Embrace failure. Leaders sometimes fail because they take risks; more often it is because they do not take risks. Failure isn't terminal; it's a launching pad. It's what you do after you get knocked down that counts. Courage matters.

- Develop a high tolerance for ambiguity and change—that is our world as it exists today. The continuing roots are your values.

- Keep your ego controlled. Arrogance is the best predictor of failure.

- Nourish your mind, your body and your spirit continuously.

- If it matters, make it happen. Challenge the impossible or the difficult. Break down the walls to make what is right a reality.

- Make sure you make priorities of the things that count in your life and in your organization. You can control more than you dream…and dream a lot.

In this third chapter—also the third step in our five-step system for achieving greater career success—we have discussed the importance of positioning your profile to take advantage of the supply and demand dynamics of the talent market. We reviewed the importance of differentiated market positioning and also discussed the benefits of moving across industry sectors to better leverage your experience and skill sets. Lastly, we discussed the cultivation of effective leadership as a means for further differentiating your profile.

Key Chapter Takeaways

» The principles of supply and demand in the talent market have a direct and considerable impact on your career development.

» Positioning yourself in growth sectors with higher demand and a limited supply of talent results in less competition for open positions, greater opportunity to build accomplishments, more rapid advancement, and enhanced compensation leverage.

» Be mindful of building experiences and skill sets that will differentiate your profile in the market.

» To reach the C-suite, you will need to become a recognized leader. Become an ongoing student of effective leadership. Seek out and embrace opportunities to be a leader.

Notes:

4

STEP FOUR

Build an Attractive
Executive Profile

**"Without continual growth and progress,
such words as improvement, achievement, and
success have no meaning."** — *Benjamin Franklin*

"What specifically makes an executive an attractive candidate?"

"How can I improve my attractiveness in the employment market?"

These are two questions I am frequently asked by business professionals. In order to answer these questions, you need to understand first what employers are seeking, and second, to what degree you possess what they are seeking. It seems pretty straight-forward. However, it requires honest, objective self-reflection and knowledge as well as an understanding of the key characteristics employers are assessing among their pool of potential candidates. Companies are looking at many aspects of your executive profile to obtain a complete picture of you as a potential hire. Your unique combination of skills, knowledge, experience, and interpersonal traits all contribute to forming your own unique executive profile.

Through my many years of experience as an executive search consultant at Spencer Stuart, I gained valuable insights into what corporate clients assess in finalizing their hiring decisions. Based on these accumulated observations, I have developed a list of 10 Key Components that determine a candidate's overall attractiveness to potential employers. The degree to which you exhibit positive in each of these components will determine the attrac- your executive profile. When assessing executives, I ιοι̣ nderstanding the strength of these components to deter- mine the attractiveness of their candidacy relative to other execu- tives being considered. Below I describe these 10 Key Components:

1. **Experience**—a combination of acquired skill sets, knowledge and experiences that positively differentiate your ability to be successful in a given role

2. **Impact**—the results you achieve, the positive effect you have on results, activities and those who you work with directly and indirectly

3. **Potential**—the pace of your career and what it says about your future. Are you on the fast track, progressive track, or have you stalled in the same position at one or numerous organizations?

4. **Stability**—or tenure within organizations is a reflection of your ability to integrate effectively and be accepted, make contributions and build productive work relationships over a minimum of three to five years on average

5. **Quality**—the quality of the companies, organizations, and people with whom you have worked

6. **Presence**—the confidence, composure, credibility and temperament to positively connect with others

7. **Passion**—your perceived energy, enthusiasm, excitement and commitment

8. **Influence**—the ability to effectively have an impact on your surroundings, assert yourself, collaborate, build teams, and create followers who support an organization's mission

9. **Intelligence**—a composite of your innate intelligence, emotional intelligence, street smarts, and learning agility, as well as academic performance, level of education, course selection, and quality of educational institutions. Intelligence is an indicator of problem solving skills and ability to identify opportunities through the assimilation of information.

10. **Reputation**—the result of your cumulative interactions
    with others over time, both professionally and personally.
    Reputation is a reflection of the quality and outcomes of your
    work, your interpersonal relationships, and the integrity you
    have shown.

Establish Your EPAM—Executive Profile Attractiveness Measure

EPAM (Executive Profile Attractiveness Measure) is an assessment
tool I developed to help professionals take an honest look at their
strengths and weaknesses with regard to the 10 Key Components
highlighted above. Before we dive more deeply into each of the 10
components and discuss actions you can take to strengthen your
profile, I would like you to stop and quickly take this assessment
to get your EPAM score. This is a learning tool; there's no right or
wrong. The more honest you are about your strengths and weaknesses, the more you will get out of this exercise and the following
pages. Here's how it works:

Step One: Establish Your EPAM

Under each of the 10 Key Components below, rate yourself as
objectively as possible on a scale of 1-low to 10-high. Refer to the
accompanying bullet points to help you arrive at a rating. Mark
your rating in the space provided on the right side of the page.
Remember, be as honest and objective as possible. Otherwise, the
results of this exercise will have less value in helping you build a
strong executive profile.

1. Experience / Score: _____

- My collective experience, skill sets, and knowledge are valued
  by my company.

- I have developed a valuable range of experiences that is
  in demand, and which positions me in a productive and
  differentiated manner in the market.

- My experience is current with emerging trends in my industry and I am well positioned for the future.

2. Impact / Score: _____

- I have taken on positions of meaningful responsibility and made contributions that have materially impacted the performance of the organizations with which I've worked.

- The positive impact of these contributions would not have occurred without my involvement.

3. Potential / Score: _____

- I have repeatedly taken on new or larger responsibilities as a result of strong prior performance.

- I seek out challenges that provide me new learning opportunities and broader exposure.

- I have adapted well to new situations and come up to speed quickly.

4. Stability / Score: _____

- My profile shows that I have not "job hopped" and that I have been able to receive promotions within the same company.

- My average tenure with an employer is 4-5 years or more.

5. Quality / Score: _____

- I have worked with recognized and respected companies that are market leaders with a reputation for attracting great talent, having respected senior management, favorable performance records, innovation and positive cultures.

6. Presence / Score: _____

- I make a positive and credible first impression and exhibit an optimistic and confident attitude.

- I possess well-developed listening skills and am able to communicate in a highly effective and engaging manner through the written word, orally person-to-person, and in both small and large groups.

- I am a compelling presenter to larger audiences.

7. Passion / Score: _____

- While operating day-to-day, I outwardly exhibit energy and observable passion and commitment for what I am doing and my business.
- I am able to engage others through my enthusiasm.

8. Influence / Score: _____

- My experience, skill sets and knowledge are respected and enable me to have an impact on what is going on around me within the organization.
- Others look to me for my support, thoughts, and guidance.
- I have built effective internal relationships in my company with peers, subordinates, and managers above me and consistently influence their thinking.
- I am able to bring people together, articulate a course of action, organize around stated objectives, and drive execution.
- Others in the organization are responsive to me.

9. Intelligence / Score: _____

- I have exhibited an uncommon level of intelligence (illustrated by either complex problem solving, academic achievement, or intelligence testing).
- I am someone who others describe as a "quick study"—able to adapt to and learn in new environments and make a positive impact.

10. Reputation / Score: _____

- I have a broad and very positive reputation for doing great work, having high integrity, consistently achieving results, and being someone with whom others want to work.
- If asked at this minute, I am able to provide at least six references from a combination of my current and former employers who will enthusiastically attest to my work, integrity, results, and ability to work with others.

Step Two: Calculate Your EPAM

Once you have objectively and honestly rated your profile across these ten dimensions on the 1-low to 10-high point scale, add the numbers to arrive at your total EPAM score.

Total EPAM Score: _____

Step Three: Assess Your EPAM

Compare your total score to the EPAM ranges provided below. Your score will provide you with an initial appreciation for how attractive your current executive profile is to recruiters and in the job market. After this section, we'll delve into each of the 10 components to discover how you can strengthen areas of weakness and put a spotlight on your strengths to establish a highly competitive and attractive executive profile.

Here is what your EPAM tells you:

85-100 points: You have a very good to excellent profile and are well on your way to optimizing your inherent capabilities, intellect and experience. If you continue to manage and position your career and profile successfully, you should have attractive future opportunities and increased compensation. Executive recruiters will want to have you on their radar. Be selective in choosing the recruiters you work with. Identify those who are doing work in the functions and industry sectors you are interested in. Get to know them, and let them get to know you. Stay in touch.

70-84 points: You have a solid to good profile, but should determine whether you can improve the dimensions where you are less developed. Assuming that the skills and experience you do have match the specific job requirements, you are a reasonable to good candidate in the eyes of executive recruiters. Be aware that you will likely find stiff competition for the most attractive roles, so continued development is advised.

50-69 points: You have considerable opportunity to improve the attractiveness of your profile. This might be because you are early in your career, or you have not been mindful of managing your career to develop requisite skills, experience, and track record that you need in order to be highly competitive. Your current profile does not effectively distinguish you from others. As such, you are likely losing the ability to leverage your profile for new roles and higher compensation. Focus on those dimensions where you are least developed. Seek out the guidance of trusted colleagues, a mentor or a career coach.

35-40 points: You have a lot of opportunity to improve, either because you are very early in your career, or you have recently made a transition into a very different arena. It is also possible that you have not had the flexibility or inclination to build an attractive profile. In either case, you substantially lack the necessary skill sets, knowledge and experience that recruiters and employers are looking for. If your career is important to you or others, you need to establish an action-oriented game plan to enrich the ten Key Components described in this chapter. Unless you do this, you will find that your future options are limited.

Below 35 points: Unless you are just starting out your career, you need to undertake some serious self-reflection and determine whether you are on the right career track. There may be other roles that will be a more comfortable fit with who you are. You will likely want to consider further training as well.

Step Four: Strengthen Your Executive Profile Based on Your EPAM

Having now completed the EPAM self-diagnostic questionnaire, let's dig deeper into each of the 10 Key Components of your executive profile, explore how to improve the lesser-developed areas and further develop your strengths.

Building the 10 Key Components of Your Executive Profile

The following material is intended to provide further context around building the key components of an attractive executive profile and to provide practical suggestions for how to further strengthen each of these dimensions.

1. Experience

The top component assessed by recruiters and potential employers is relevant experience. The roles you have previously held define not only your experience, skill sets and knowledge but also serve to differentiate your positioning in the job market. Your resume—a chronology of your experiences—is a strong indicator of your ability to be successful in the new role you are being considered for. Most executive profiles will have a core skill or competency around which other supplemental skills and competencies are added over time. Your core competency often becomes the common thread of your professional career. Increasingly today, these core skills have a technical, critical thinking or interpersonal dimension.

> Your core competency often becomes the common thread of your professional career.

Four years ago I placed an executive named Robert into a national mutual insurance company as SVP Customer Insights & Analytics. He was hired to build an enterprise-wide data and analytics function by centralizing the company's research, analytics, strategy support, forecasting, data and information management activities. Over the ensuing five years, Robert built a talented staff of 160 professionals and oversaw a budget of $100 million a year in research and analytic expenditures. His earlier background as Executive Director of Research and Forecasting at a global automotive company was not an obvious fit for the role. However, Robert's prior seven years of experience as a Research Officer and Senior Economist with the Federal Reserve Bank, followed by four years of consulting and six years of running a sizeable research and forecasting group at the automotive company, provided the core skill sets to be successful in a large insurance company. He and I recognized that the core underpinning of his profile—a strong quantitative and technical acumen—combined with his management strengths and experiences, would enable him to find success in a new industry sector. In fact, this proved to be the case.

If the "Experience" component of your profile is in need of development or you would like to further leverage this dimension of your professional profile, here are some ideas:

- Identify your core skills or competencies, in other words, your foundational strengths. Foundational strengths and skill sets are the learned or innate abilities that you possess which represent the professional core of who you are. These are the abilities that allow you to add value. You will rely on them throughout your career. Examine your history from adolescence to present to identify what it is that you do consistently and naturally better than others. Ask others you have worked closely with to help you identify two or three of your most pronounced foundational skills or competencies. Use this feedback to further build this dimension of your profile and focus your career around these strengths.

- Volunteer for new assignments, projects, committees, and the challenges not pursued by others at your company. Doing this will broaden your skill sets, experience, areas of knowledge, and contacts as well as establish you as a "go-to" person. Furthermore, you will find new ways to leverage your strongest competencies and, along the way, develop a more holistic sense of your organization.

- Never stop learning! Attend industry conferences and training seminars. Participate in industry associations that allow you to interface with and learn from peers. Study analogous businesses or similar industries. Occasionally, take some time to step outside of your primary functional expertise or industry and spend time reading or interacting with others to learn about different job functions or industries. This added perspective will enable you to become a better rounded executive. You may even identify an emerging industry or function where your key skill sets and experience can be well applied.

- Have an articulated goal in mind for your career. Don't drift aimlessly. Talk with others to define the particular experiences and knowledge gaps you need to fill in order to reach your career objective. Let others know your desire (i.e., friends, peers in the industry, recruiters, and a mentor within your organization, if appropriate). It is difficult for others to assist you if they do not understand what you want. Don't be afraid to redefine your career goals as life unfolds. Aligning your skills and competencies into scenarios where they will be leveraged allows them to more fully develop.

- Identify new, emerging skill and knowledge requirements arising in the market and seek experiences that allow you to obtain this understanding and proficiency. For example, if you are a marketer, you will want to develop a familiarity with how and when to leverage Big Data, social media, mobile advertising, and Artificial Intelligence. You do not necessarily have to know the technical detail or software programming required, but you do need to understand how to use these newer technologies beneficially.

- Develop a key reading list of relevant publications (industry magazines, websites, journals, published studies). Potential topics might include leadership, motivating teams, negotiating, and management. Apply this learning in your day-to-day activities. A curious mind is a tremendous asset for building and strategically shaping your experience.

- Enlist the support of third parties affiliated with your organization who can help fill in your experience and knowledge gaps. For example, a marketing professional might leverage and absorb the knowledge and understanding of his or her advertising agency, media buying agency, market research provider, and digital/website developer.

2. Impact

Your value and upward mobility in an organization is directly correlated to the results you achieve, your impact on others in your organization, and the contributions you make outside of your immediate role.

Over the years, I've seen many resumes that do not adequately highlight meaningful professional achievements. This occurs either because the resume is too heavily focused on describing responsibilities and details of specific roles as opposed to outcomes, or the individual in fact had little impact while he or she was in the role. If you have generated concrete results in a position, you need to highlight those results on your resume, preferably in measurable terms. If you do not have results to highlight, you need to refocus your activities and find opportunities to make an impact.

Years ago a former candidate, who we'll call Sarah, was interested in a search assignment we were conducting for a client. Sarah was a particularly talented senior account director at an advertising agency. We agreed to present her resume as part of a long list of prospective candidates for the role. Her resume did a nice job of describing her day-to-day activities and listing the many clients with whom she had worked. However, missing was crucial information concerning the impact of her billings and ad campaigns. There was little mention of the challenges and issues that she had helped to resolve for her company and clients. Her resume did not stand out from others in the long list presented to my client. As a result, the client did not select her background for further consideration. Having spent considerable time getting to know Sarah, I believed in her candidacy and asked her to do some research and highlight the impact of her ad campaigns in terms of increases in brand awareness, trial and incremental revenue gains. This additional information led my client to reconsider her profile, meet her, and ultimately offer her the position. She accepted the offer and became Head of Advertising for a Midwest greeting card company.

Here are some helpful suggestions for developing the "Impact" component of your profile:

- Focus your activities on initiatives and projects that will enable you to have a meaningful impact on outcomes.

- Create and present proposals and action plans within your company that will have measurable results. This will make it easier for you to quantify impact on your resume.

- Develop a broader perspective and influence beyond your immediate role. Understand the priorities, key challenges, issues and opportunities your organization and industry face. One way this can be accomplished is to proactively volunteer for committees and multi-functional task forces that have been convened to tackle key opportunities and issues. This will allow you to become more broadly recognized for your contributions. Attending industry conferences is another way to broaden your perspective. It will also help you learn how to better anticipate business issues and potential solutions in your industry.

- Understand how your performance is going to be evaluated as well as your organization's key priorities. Set achievable objectives that stretch your abilities. Then, meet or exceed those objectives.

- Be visible in working towards results. Collaborate with others and keep your manager apprised of your progress. If you accomplish your goals in a vacuum, no one will know.

- Understand which areas of your organization are receiving funding and get involved in those areas. It is a lot easier to create an impact when you have resources.

- Keep a list of achievements and contributions that you have driven or been a part of throughout the year. Adding to this list should be easy and not require a lot of time. This exercise is helpful at year-end when you are preparing for your performance review. It will also make the process of periodically updating your resume more efficient.

3. Potential

Typically, the first step taken by a recruiter or employer is to review your resume. He or she will determine if you are a "fit" for the job and assess your career trajectory—whether you are on a fast track, progressive track, or have stalled in the same position at one or several organizations. One approximate measure of your career progression is the ratio of your total compensation to your current age, relative to your professional peers. The reason your track record is of interest to recruiters and employers is that it is an indication of your future potential.

> The reason your track record is of interest to recruiters and employers is that it is an indication of your future potential.

Trajectory is not necessarily a linear function. There will be times during your career when you will deliberately choose to move more slowly through an organization or job change. There may also be periods when you move more quickly. Most careers have detours and setbacks. What's important is the persistence, determination, and GRIT (guts, resilience, initiative, tenacity) that you show in getting back on track. Often, an executive who exhibits a slower track in one particular function or setting can rejuvenate his or her trajectory in another function, company, or industry that is better suited to his or her skills, interests and goals.

Early in my career, I worked with an executive who I'll call John. John was a senior brand-marketing manager at a consumer goods company. He was especially gifted with quantitative skills and considered an opportunity outside the marketing function within the organization. John accepted this role in the company's operations planning function as a group manager. Many of his peers viewed this move out of marketing to be undesirable and a mistake. However, the operational understanding that John developed in this position added a unique dimension to his marketing background and the development of his business profile. This positioned him for future general management responsibilities at a regional, divisional, and ultimately CEO level. He went on to run businesses ranging in size from $300 million to $1 billion. Reflecting these increases in responsibility, John's base, bonus, and equity compensation increased to over $1 million annually. He went on to work in private equity, where his operational background and analytical skills continued to serve him well and provided him with equity ownership in small and mid-cap companies that were being built.

Such good fortune occurs more frequently when you understand your strengths and take the time to make smart decisions to differentiate your career track—as John did. The earlier you recognize your strengths, the more opportunities you will have to leverage them in building a differentiated profile that benefits your career progression. Here are some further suggestions for demonstrating and building your "Potential" in the job market:

- Consciously build your resume throughout your career and seek responsibilities and activities that allow you to fill in gaps in your professional profile. This requires forethought, research and asking for such opportunities.

- Work to earn several job promotions within a single company. When someone consistently shows a track record of having to change companies in order to receive a title increase, it raises a red flag.

- Work with organizations that ideally are in a growth mode and have a clear and distinct need for your skills. Seek to fill organizational "voids" where your core skills can be fully utilized. This will allow you to more readily contribute, show accomplishments and be positioned for promotions.

- If your current responsibilities are being well handled, ask your superior for additional responsibilities. This lets others know that you are eager to learn new skills and contribute in new ways to the organization. It also increases awareness of your potential.

- Starting your career with larger, blue chip organizations or more rapidly growing mid-sized companies can offer stronger initial training, development, and alternative career paths. I believe that it is easier to start your career with larger companies and go smaller rather than start small and go large. Additionally, learning to navigate your way through a larger, matrixed organization structure helps build valuable influencing skills.

- Enrich the substance of your background by accepting lateral roles into new divisions and functions or an international assignment. This will allow you to further distinguish your profile versus those of your peers. Doing these things successfully showcases your ability to learn, adapt, and influence in different settings, roles and businesses. Individuals who show learning agility and adaptability tend to be considered for a broader range of opportunities and are more apt to transition their skill sets into other industry sectors.

- To develop a general management profile, seek activities and roles that provide you breadth as well as depth of understanding across multiple functions. This might include roles in sales, marketing, product development, customer service, manufacturing or service delivery, strategic planning, and finance/corporate development. Additionally, experience in both line and staff functions provides additional breadth of perspective.

4. Stability

How is the concept of job "stability" an influence on your career? First, frequent job moves to different companies will raise red flags for recruiters and employers. These red flags raise questions about your durability, effectiveness, loyalty, or interpersonal skills. Second, on the other hand, too much stability may be interpreted as a lack of ambition. Long tenure used to be viewed more positively than it is today. Potential employers may look at lengthy tenure and be skeptical about your ability to transition into a new company, provide a broad and well-rounded perspective, and learn new systems and processes.

One executive I had known for years—let's call him Jake—was a very competent Internet/ecommerce executive. However, he became impatient with his career and made a series of four rapid, poorly considered moves in just five years. These rapid moves made it difficult for him to demonstrate long-term impact in any of his recent positions. Our executive search clients showed great reluctance to consider his background because of this. Jake ultimately did land a promising role with a Midwest specialty retailer, selling apparel online in 20 countries. Within several years after starting this role, Jake contacted me and explained that he was interested in making another move. I explained that in good conscience I would not present him because the best move for him was to stay with his current company long enough to show stability, results, increased responsibilities, and ideally a promotion or two. He did listen, understood this, and reluctantly did so.

Jake has now been at this company for over seven years. He has been promoted to Senior Vice President of Marketing, eCommerce and Corporate Development, and is earning roughly $1 million annually—300% higher than when he left his prior company. He oversees 8 people directly and manages a global team of 200 and has full P&L responsibility. Jake is a member of the 10-person executive committee, reports directly to the CEO, and is today managing a $1 billion revenue. More importantly, he has added an important attribute of stability to his profile. As a result, the attractiveness of his background is demonstrably greater than it was when he came to me. Clearly, there are times when you need to be patient with your career.

If you would like to strengthen the "Stability" component of your executive profile, here are some suggestions:

- Choose to work with growing organizations that enjoy strong balance sheets, stable and respected leadership, healthy cultures, and a pronounced need for your skill sets. You are much more likely to stay with such organizations for multiple years.

- Develop strong internal relationships and be seen as someone who is easy to work with and who gets the job done. Nothing promotes stability of employment better than strong performance and building great work relationships.

■ Make your boss look like a star and make his or her job easier.

■ Do not job hop without a very good reason. Checkerboard resumes signal to organizations that you are not a "keeper," that you have limited loyalty, or that you have faulty judgment. Employers want to be confident that you will be with their organization long enough to make their investments in you worthwhile. They will figuratively assess your value and projected rate of return.

■ Move for opportunities that will enrich your profile by allowing you to learn new skills, better position your profile, be part of a growing industry, take on greater responsibility, or be part of a great culture.

■ Switch employers thoughtfully and not just for more money or title. When assessing potential moves, consider the company's reputation, the chemistry you have with the team (especially your boss), and the fit of your skill sets and experience relative to the job that needs to be done. Additionally, understand the rate of turnover in the employee base. If it's high, this could be a warning flag. Research the cause of this turnover as best you can.

■ Identify and speak to others who have worked for the company, both present and past. LinkedIn is a very useful tool for accomplishing this. Visit Glassdoor.com to see how others rate the organization and speak about their experience there. Read the reviews to develop a directional impression, not absolute. Employees who have been asked to leave a company and are provided a venue (Glassdoor.com) to air dirty laundry can do so without proper objectivity.

■ Don't stay with the same organization for too long, as this also presents potential pitfalls. Future employers may be concerned that you have not shown an ability to transition and adapt. They may view your experience as being narrow compared to an individual who has worked in several different organizations. This concern can be mitigated if you showcase a variety of different assignments and challenges within a single organization. There is a certain richness that develops in professionals who have spent time wisely in several well-regarded and different types of organizations—for example, large and small entities, both public and private. Having this variety of experience expands the array of opportunities that you can be considered for in the future. Of course, such transitions should be fully researched and considered with the risks acknowledged.

- Seek out roles internally that cast you into new and challenging, or culturally and operationally different settings. This is especially true if you are planning to stay in your current organization for a longer period of time because either you are so content, see no better external opportunities, are waiting for children to reach a certain age or schooling, or your spouse has constraints. There are obvious exceptions that run counter to the perception of "staying too long" or being "too stable". For example, this perception does not typically apply to entrepreneurial founders, business owners or professionals who have built private practices, such as physicians, dentists, and lawyers. In fact, stability in their professions signals proven experience, trust, and success.

5. Quality

The quality of your resume and background is often judged by the excellence of the companies and organizations that it includes. Respected organizations can be either large, mid-sized or smaller. Their hallmark is that they are recognized as leaders in their industries in terms of quality, growth, financial performance or innovation. The thinking of such quality companies is progressive and the organization has a reputation for attracting exceptional talent. If you have shown advancement at several high-quality companies in your career, this will be considered a strength by recruiters and potential employers. However, throughout your career, you can afford to include several lesser recognized or lower quality organizations on your resume. The caveat here is that you must be able to explain the role that these companies played in helping you build a stronger professional profile. Also keep in mind that too many of these organizations on your resume will dilute the attractiveness of your profile.

Four years ago, I conducted a search for a Midwest-based VP of Product Development and Innovation for a multinational (Asia, North America, and Europe) European manufacturer of home and garden implements. The position was attractive to a number of strong candidates. The two finalists for the position were very well qualified and both wanted the job badly. The primary distinction between the two candidates was the perceived quality of the companies in which they had recently worked. One had started his career with several strong, respected organizations, but had been working with less highly regarded companies in recent years. The candidate who received and accepted the offer had started his career with Armstrong World Industries, then spent the next seventeen years at Whirlpool Corporation, and the most recent five years at Carrier Corporation. These were company names broadly recognized across different regions of the globe and highly regarded for their product innovations. As I noted, the candidate with the top-tier companies on his resume received the job offer. Quality matters.

Be selective in your career choices. You should carefully research and evaluate the companies you interview with just as thoroughly as they are assessing you. Understand their relative reputation and position within their industry. You do not want to be forced to make another move in one or two years simply because you "didn't know" what was happening to or in a company. As you consider potential job opportunities, keep these following tips in mind to help manage the "Quality" component of your profile:

- Some organizations which are generally perceived as being of high quality to the outside world can be very different once you get inside. Talk with those who are both inside the organization as well as those who have recently left. Check online for news of management turnover or impending mergers. Also, be aware that while a large multinational company might have a strong general reputation, the "quality"—the people, environment, culture and performance across different operating units—can vary substantially.

■ Unless you are in dire straits, do not feel that you need to sacrifice quality by accepting the first opportunity that comes your way. Take the necessary time to explore multiple options and make a decision that is right for you and your career. By exploring multiple opportunities, you will be in a better position to recognize what is most appealing about each. Should you receive an offer of employment while still assessing other attractive roles, ask for more time to come to a final decision, or play for more time by scheduling a future date to take your spouse to the new location for a look at schools and real estate—a very reasonable request. Beware of joining a company that puts unreasonable time constraints on accepting its offer of employment as this could be symptomatic of how it treats its employees. Do not be pushed into a decision if your mind, intuition, or family are not reasonably comfortable with the decision.

■ One question I've been asked repeatedly is whether a subordinate should follow his or her boss to a new company. The answer depends on how you are feeling about your current role and company, how long you have been there, and the growth and advancement prospects at your current company. If these are favorable, there is less of a reason to switch, and a greater degree of risk in moving. If they are unfavorable, you may want to entertain your prior boss's overture, depending on the nature of the new role and company. You will also want to consider your prior boss's stability and track record throughout his or her career. If he or she has a history of more rapid moves, there is greater risk in moving with him or her. Before making such a move, consider the vitality of the new company and whether the move is additive to your profile and offers opportunities to build new skills and abilities. Ask yourself whether the move will allow you to enhance your positioning in the market.

6. Presence

Your presence is a reflection of your interpersonal and communication skills (both group and one-on-one), confidence, energy, passion, and your knowledge and experience. Presence is the ability to connect with others in a credible and influential manner. I have met a number of smart and talented executives with strong minds and enviable professional achievements who fall short on the presence component and ability to engage meaningfully with others. This inability to credibly connect with others results in these professionals never quite receiving the full, enthusiastic endorsement of superiors and peers. Why? Usually because something in their demeanor, communication, or written or oral presentation skills is inconsistent with the environment they are in. While many of these professionals have a favorable start to their careers due to sheer technical competence, they find that further advancement is slowed or limited due to a lack of presence that is expected of them in order to succeed at the next level.

Executives with more introverted personalities need to work especially hard to develop a confident presence. I recall my recent experience with one mid-career executive who I will refer to as Sam. He was a very bright and well-educated professional with several impressive degrees. Sam was especially gifted quantitatively and had built powerful analytic capabilities and teams at several organizations. He was feeling that his current company was not large enough to provide further advancement opportunities and career growth. In other words, he was bottle-necked.

He also had a desire to return to the East Coast. Sam's experience and resume were attracting interest from potential employers, however, he had interviewed for seven different opportunities and not advanced into further discussions as a finalist. Sam attended one of my "How to Optimize Your Career" seminars and later approached me for more intensive and personal one-on-one coaching. I met with Sam on an exploratory basis to determine whether I was confident that I could help him. During this meeting, it became apparent that Sam tended to be more on the introverted end of the scale—not establishing consistent eye contact when he was actively thinking and talking, exhibiting a very even-keel temperament, and a communication pattern that wandered given his active mind and deep knowledge base. These tendencies caused him to come across as not fully engaged in the conversation, having lower energy and with insufficient clarity of thinking when answering interview questions. In short, he was not connecting and engaging sufficiently with key decision makers. His qualifications were strong, but his presence needed work. I explained this to him and suggested that if he really wanted to improve and was willing to focus and put in the required energy to change, that I'd try and help him. I also felt strongly that he would benefit in his current role by improving his day-to-day presence.

Sam and I have worked together over a period of five weeks. During this timeframe, he has made remarkable improvement in eye contact. To accomplish this, I initially requested that, if he could not look me in the eyes during a discussion, to come close by focusing on my forehead (a less intimidating request). Every time his eyes would wander, I would point to my forehead and he would redirect his attention. He made remarkable improvement in a short time simply by becoming more conscious of this behavior. We then focused on kicking up his energy level and exhibiting more passion for the profession that he loves within a range that was still acceptable to his comfort zone. When we role-played in mock interviews, I requested that he exhibit a level of energy and passion beyond where he would normally be comfortable.

Concurrently, we have established a crisp and compelling executive summary of his experience and profile (an elevator pitch), which he committed to memory. We further identified those talking points of his background which would be most relevant for the roles he was interested in. Finally, based off the specification for a current opportunity he is especially interested in, we anticipated what potential interview questions might be and role-played in order to allow Sam to build greater confidence. Sam progressed through multiple rounds of interviews and received a formal job offer for a role that is several times larger than his current.

⁞ ⁞ ⁞ ⁞

Another executive, a woman who I'll identify as Christine, was a young, bright and knowledgeable marketer who had joined a large, recognized printing company four years prior. This company put a premium on presence, executive stature, and the ability to project confidence. She came to me saying she was frustrated that her responsibilities had not expanded. During our discussion, she shared with me that she became visibly nervous in formal, large group presentations. Her nervous performance in these scenarios was interpreted as a lack of confidence and overshadowed the sound quality of her thinking.

Christine explained that she did not have this issue in one-on-one and smaller group presentations. She also commented that she was unsure that she would ever become comfortable thinking on her feet in front of large groups. I suggested that she might be more comfortable in smaller to mid-sized companies where there is often less formality and fewer large group presentations. Over the ensuing six months, Christine thought further about this and determined that her style, natural abilities and inclinations were a better fit for these smaller to mid-sized environments. She moved to a mid-sized, less formal organization

> During our discussion, she shared with me that she became visibly nervous in formal, large group presentations.

where she was able to get a fresh start in a more comfortable environment. The strength of her thinking and higher level of comfort and confidence in small group and one-on-one interactions enabled her to establish more credible presence and take on added responsibilities in the ensuing four years.

The lessons in this example are: 1) Presence does significantly impact your credibility and how others view, accept and respond to you and 2) There are settings, situations, and cultures where your unique presence will more naturally shine than others. This notion of "fit" is something you should consider when exploring job opportunities.

Here are some further thoughts and insights that may help you enhance the "Presence" dimension of your profile:

- Assuming you have a lot of the "right stuff," your ability to present and connect effectively in one-on-one, small group, and large group settings will carry great weight and influence regarding how others perceive you. If you engage and connect with your audience, a modest idea presented with conviction and persuasiveness can trump a good idea that is ineffectively presented. Create opportunities to present in venues and to audiences you are comfortable communicating with (peers, suppliers, customers, and your boss) in order to build your confidence and credibility.

- Practice is the best way to improve your ability to connect, present and build presence. If you were one of the fortunate few who had the foresight to join your high school debate team or be in theatrical performances, congratulations. You received a lot of valuable training very early in your career. If you worked in a management consulting firm or ad agency where you had to formally present to senior client executives on a regular basis, you too are lucky. That's great training as well. Presence and communication are likely second nature to both of these groups.

- If you have not had such early training, go in search of it. Become as comfortable and skilled in these scenarios as early in your career as possible. Finding opportunities to build your interpersonal, presentation and oral and written communication skills may require you to insert yourself into some uncomfortable situations. Most likely, you're going to have to force yourself out of your comfort zone while you pursue development of these skills. It will be worth the effort. Great presentations inspire others to believe in you and seek you out. Coworkers and superiors will want you on their team. Your reputation as a strong communicator will grow.

■ If you are having trouble finding opportunities in your current organization to strengthen your presentation skills, you may want to sign up for a local acting or comedy class. Not only will you improve your stage presence, you'll also have some fun and make some new friends. Taking a leadership role in a local non-profit organization can also provide opportunities to develop your presentation and communication skills. Presentation presence is an important element in a well-developed professional profile. Identify your weaknesses in this area and seek opportunities—either inside or outside your organization—to strengthen those skills. This is especially important for those who aspire to executive leadership positions where strong presence is a basic requirement.

■ How else can you practice? Join a speakers group like Toastmasters International. There are chapters in many cities. Study other individuals as they present, whether within your company or outside. Volunteer to participate in Industry Association Panel Discussions or lead seminars on topics which you are comfortable with. Create venues for bringing together executives to discuss current topics of interest. Watch TED talks. Better yet, give a TED talk.

■ In many roles, your ability to artfully express yourself in the written word is critical if your plans and recommendation are to be received and seriously considered. If your writing skills are not sufficient, tackle this shortcoming early in your career. Gather and study examples of well-written documents within your company, enroll in a writing course, ask others who write well to review some of your written work. Inadequate writing skills diminish your clarity of thought as well as your credibility. Amazon Founder and CEO Jeff Bezos values writing over talking so much so that in Amazon senior executive meetings, "before any conversation or discussion begins, everyone sits for 30 minutes in total silence, carefully reading six-page printed memos." "There is no way to write a six-page, narratively structured memo and not have clear thinking," Bezos has said.

- Odds are that many of your colleagues are capable presenters, but not outstanding. You should strive to be outstanding. Do you come across in a positive, confident, interesting and credible manner in one-on-one and group interactions? If you do, others will want to be part of your success.

7. Passion

A candidate's passion, energy and commitment go a long way with recruiters and potential employers. These three traits are interrelated and critical to significant achievement in your career. Would you rather team with someone who shows energy and excitement about what they do or someone who appears to be going through the motions? Would you rather follow a leader who acts with passion and commitment, or a leader who is noncommittal and robotic in their pursuit of goals?

A story about a woman I'll refer to as Jane perfectly demonstrates the power of energy, passion and commitment. I placed Jane in a position as CEO of a privately held $120 million underperforming consumer products business on the East Coast. The business was largely a direct mail driven model with a dated product and an aging consumer base. Jane had previously been a Division President, but never a standalone CEO. However, she had a burning desire to prove herself in a CEO role.

This burning desire to succeed in her initial CEO role fueled an extraordinary level of energy, commitment, and passion that was contagious throughout the organization. In very short order, she inspired and led the development of a strategic plan that included building and launching a brand of contemporary products in new channels while preserving the cash-rich legacy business. In less than three years, she rebranded the company, built an ecommerce business, successfully sold product on QVC in the U.S. and U.K., saved over $6 million through disciplined P&L management, led manufacturing's conversion to six sigma production, introduced a professional product development methodology that included ethnographic research and qualitative/quantitative tools, developed an emotion/needs-based brand architecture, and hired needed senior managers to the team. As a result, she and her team revitalized a broken business model and provided strategic options for the company's investors. This revitalization would not have been possible without her tremendous energy, passion, focus, and commitment. The example she set inspired peak performance from her team while simultaneously strengthening her professional profile tenfold.

Here are some ideas to strengthen the "Passion" component of your profile:

- When you talk about your job to someone, do he or she come away saying, "Wow, you clearly love what you do?" Energy and passion should flow quite naturally through you, if you are in the right profession and role. Hopefully, you are. If not, life is too short to spend time doing something you have limited interest in doing. Take the time to assess your interests and skills and align them with a career that provides meaning and fulfillment. These will inspire passion.

- Maybe it is not in your nature to visibly exhibit energy or passion. I don't accept this. Learning how to show some passion is better than showing little! A good way to become more aware of how you come across to others is to tape record your phone conversations or videotape a presentation. I did this early in my career at someone's suggestion. It really hit me between the eyes. You can improve the way you communicate dramatically, if you pay attention to your communication style. Similar to learning anything new, you just have to practice until your new communication style becomes habit. Your goal is to come across to others in a committed, high-energy manner—focused, action-oriented and confident. You want to come across as well-reasoned and well-informed. You want to engage others with your passion and sense of purpose. Identify others in your company who exhibit these traits and who generate energy, passion, and commitment in others. Watch how they interact with others and in meetings. Adopt and practice their behaviors. It might feel awkward at first, but with time it will become natural.

- If you're still not convinced what an impact passion, energy and commitment make, try an experiment. Try interacting with your spouse or girlfriend or boyfriend in a low passion, energy and commitment mode. The following day, try interacting with that same person in a high passion, energy and commitment mode. How much of a different reaction and response do you receive?

8. Influence

The more senior your role in an organization, the more you will rely on and work through others to get things done. Your success—regardless of how smart and confident you are—will become increasingly dependent on the cooperation and success of others. Consequently, your influencing, collaboration and leadership skills will become increasingly important. In this regard, you'll need to demonstrate that you have the ability to forge productive interpersonal relationships, team with others effectively, shape the thinking and actions of colleagues, build and lead and motivate groups, and navigate the complexities of an organization.

I recall meeting with an experienced sales executive who I'll refer to as Jim. Jim had received strong initial training from an academy company (a company known for exceptional training and strong sales talent) in the technology sector. As a solitary, individual contributor, Jim had an impressive track record and was making very good money thanks to his company's commission structure. However, he had not succeeded in the same manner after being promoted to a sales manager role two years prior, and was told that he had likely gone as far as he could in management due to lack of collaboration, team building and organizational skills.

As we sat and talked, I learned that Jim had been an accomplished high school wrestler who came from a family that was intensely competitive. His will to "win" had driven him to excel in wrestling and to do well in school. Success was seen to be the result of hard work, focus, and discipline. When he met barriers, Jim would overcome them through sheer persistence and force. He had limited experience leading others and working as part of a team. He took pride in his individual accomplishments versus the success of others collectively. Jim's self-awareness of how he came across in group environments, received input from others, and recognized their contributions was not well developed. It became very clear to me why he had fallen short in his initial leadership role.

I suggested to Jim that he might have to develop a very different mindset, awareness of his surroundings and his impact on others if he wanted to be an effective sales manager. We discussed team building, creating followership, listening to other points of view, and enabling the success of others. Jim decided that he would be happier and experience greater freedom as more of an individual contributor with minimal or no management responsibility. Ultimately, he found that his earnings, while good, had limited upside due to territory and commission restructuring. Had Jim developed further skill sets—including interpersonal, teaming and organizational acumen—he'd have been better positioned for a broader array of future opportunities.

Here are some ideas to consider as you work to strengthen your "Influence" skills:

- This ability comes more naturally to those who have been involved in group or team structures early in life. This can include participation in team sports such as soccer, football, baseball, basketball, and filed hockey as opposed to individual sports like wrestling, track, swimming and figure skating. It seems that the discipline and focus required for these individual pursuits does not lend itself as readily to group dynamics. If your early background focused on such individual pursuits, you may want to get involved in some group activities for learning's sake or get some coaching. Other early activities that produce influencing skills include involvement in student government, school committees, clubs and group leadership roles.

- Effective interpersonal, teaming and organizational skills—which are critical components of influence and leadership—require knowing when to speak and when to listen. Listen to yourself in different scenarios. Are you constantly in a transmit mode, or do you also have an active receiving mode? How self-aware are you in terms of how you come across to others?

- Build personal and political capital by proactively getting to know others in your organization, one on one, both within your department and outside. This also provides you with a more well-rounded view of what is going on in the organization. Don't wait for others to approach you; that may not happen. Lunches are a great way to get to know your colleagues. Building relationships requires you to be proactive, to initiate and identify opportunities for interaction. Figure out what makes others tick and what their objectives are. Be open, friendly and helpful. Ongoing communication, respect and integrity go a long way in building relationships.

- Become involved in, or form a group task force within your company to tackle a particular business problem or opportunity. You will learn from this experience. If you are uncomfortable forming such a group, suggest to a potential team member that he or she might want to form such a group and that you are able to make a valuable contribution.

- I have observed that there are distinct groups of individuals who by background or upbringing believe that if they simply work hard enough and put in extraordinarily long hours, they will get noticed and succeed. They are prone to make comments like, "I don't have time to develop relationships. My work speaks for itself." Unfortunately, while these folks typically master the technical dimensions of a role, they fall significantly short on building broad and strong internal working relationships which allow them to have greater influence. What's more, the relationships that they do build both inside and outside of the workplace tend to be with others who are quite similar to themselves.

Develop and maintain a broad perspective of how what you do fits into the remainder of the organization and how others think. Developing this understanding, these relationships and comfortable interpersonal skills puts you in a better position to influence what's going on around you. Showing that you are able to develop and manage relationships is a requirement if you intend to move into a management position where strong influencing and leadership skills are required on a daily basis.

- Give due credit to others graciously, sincerely, and as often as warranted. Let others know that you appreciate their effort and responsiveness, and how important their role is. They will be that much more willing to support you in the future.

- Offer unsolicited support. Exhibit a great attitude. Take time to explain what you are doing. Understand your role on the team and the roles of others. Show respect for all team members at all levels. Exhibit empathy and appropriate emotion when warranted. Be motivated for the good of the greater organization and others.

- Do not make your needs and personal objectives the overriding consideration. Share information. Accept and embrace accountability. Surround yourself with talented and motivated individuals. Be politically attuned, but not political.

- Do not feel that you need to show others that you are the smartest person in the room. Take time to listen to others' points of view.

9. Intelligence

When assessing the attractiveness of executive profiles, recruiters and potential employers, look for candidates who have exhibited various forms of intelligence—IQ (Intelligence Quotient), EQ (Emotional Intelligence), street smarts, and learning agility. Put simply, IQ measures your reasoning and problem-solving abilities. EQ reflects a person's ability to empathize with others: identify, evaluate, control and express your own emotions, and perceive and assess others' emotions. EQ also refers to one's ability to use emotions to facilitate thinking and understand emotional meanings. Street smarts refers to one's common sense, savvy, shrewdness, and wisdom in dealing with the world around them. Executives with strong learning agility are those individuals who are able to rapidly study, analyze, and understand new situations and new business problems. Learning agility is recognized to be an important attribute of successful senior executives.

Some obvious but imperfect indicators of "smarts" are academic performance, level of education, course selection, and quality of educational institutions. Education is an initial, but by no means complete, indicator of intelligence. Many highly competent individuals lack ideal academic credentials. Perhaps because of their upbringing, limited financial or personal resources, or due to the fact that they were the first in their family to go to college and did not receive early guidance.

> Education is an initial, but by no means complete, indicator of intelligence.

Graduating from a respected college or university can greatly facilitate an introduction or the ability to land interviews with organizations early in your career. However, it's even more important to demonstrate that you are able to apply your intelligence and education in a meaningful manner in the real world. Where you went to school becomes less important, almost a footnote, as your career progresses. I've met a number of very well educated, pedigreed and book-smart individuals who are not able to apply their education in a meaningful manner, or who have absolutely no street smarts and limited emotional intelligence. Conversely, I've met other individuals with modest education backgrounds, but who are inquisitive problem-solvers, learn quickly and are able to "read the tea leaves." Your achievements, critical thinking, track record and reputation soon overshadow your choice of educational institutions. Of course, the value of a school's alumni network over time can be a significant asset, if properly tapped. There is also a sense of pride in having a top school on your resume as a rite of passage. However, formal education is only part of your overall intelligence.

Here are some suggestions to help you further build your "Intelligence" and become more attractive to potential employers:

- If your level or quality of education does not jump off the page, this can be supplemented by additional course work or training. This can be accomplished through individual coursework in relevant and valuable subject matter or the achievement of a full advanced degree (full time or through evening studies). Investigate also whether there are certification programs relevant to your profession.

- Become a passionate life-time learner. Never stop learning. Challenge yourself. Become a voracious reader of publications relevant to your industry or job.

- Learning agility is a muscle that grows with use and experience. The more you exercise it, the easier it gets. When given the opportunity, work alongside others who have exceptional learning agility and observe their processes and approach to understanding business problems and challenges.

- Absorb the behaviors, listening skills and mindset of individuals with high emotional intelligence. What do they do that you do not? How do they react to the emotions of others? How do they diffuse tension or inspire others?

As discussed above, there are various forms of intelligence possessed by the most attractive senior executives—IQ, EQ, street smarts, and learning agility. It is important to develop yourself across each of these dimensions of intelligence. You can accomplish this by identifying opportunities to place yourself into scenarios and projects that require you to exercise each of these. The productive application of these dimensions over time will differentiate and distinguish your profile.

10. Reputation

Your reputation results directly from your cumulative interactions with others over time—both professionally and personally. It also encompasses the quality and outcomes of your professional activities and the integrity with which you have pursued these outcomes. References are essentially the embodiment of your reputation. They are essentially different sides of the same coin.

I remember during my early years with Spencer Stuart, there was a highly regarded search consultant at another firm. This individual had built an elite national reputation and was billing upwards of $2,000,000 at the time—an impressive figure back then! The company this person worked for learned that he was padding his expense account and passing these expenses on to clients. This person's departure from his employer was abrupt and word of this spread quickly. His reputation in the industry was severely damaged. This does not mean that this individual was necessarily a bad person, but that he or she had shown a lapse in judgment resulting in a perception of misplaced values and greed, which sowed mistrust. Next time your stomach is feeling uncertain about something you are about to do or say, ask yourself how others would perceive it. How would you feel tomorrow morning when you woke up and learned that your action or behavior was shared on Facebook?

Here are some other key thoughts about how to preserve and strengthen the "Reputation" component of your professional profile:

- When creating or updating your resume do not: claim degrees that you do not have, omit employers, or mislead on anything regarding positions held, accountabilities and accomplishments.

■ Always keep in mind that what others say and think about you matters a lot! You build a reputation one action, one interaction at a time—repeatedly over time.

■ Positive reputations are built deliberately with hard work and strong personal values over many years. However, a great reputation can vanish overnight due to lack of judgment. How often we've seen this very instance played out on the front page of *The Wall Street Journal*. When faced with an important decision, ask yourself, "If I did this and it were to appear on the front page of tomorrow's newspaper, would my reputation be stronger or diminished?"

■ Regarding references, do not wait until you need them to figure out who you should ask and what they will say. Instead, consciously and consistently cultivate references through your activities and the relationships you build throughout your career—both within and outside your organization. Identify several individuals who you interface with on a weekly basis and with whom you have some natural chemistry. These should be individuals who are dependent on the results of your efforts. Go out of your way to be responsive, helpful, and supportive of their goals and activities. Pre-determine specifically what you would like these individuals to say about you and then look for opportunities to shape their perceptions. Identify mutually shared business objectives. Ensure that those who report to you understand why these relationships are important to your group and maintain these activities. Periodically schedule lunches to review the status of activities and keep these potential references "in the loop."

> Regarding references, do not wait until you need them to figure out who you should ask and what they will say.

Key Chapter Takeaways:

)) Attractive executive profiles are built deliberately over time as a result of strong and consistent job performance, proactive career management, effective interpersonal relations, continuous learning, and smart job selections.

)) The 10 Key Components of your profile that determine your attractiveness to recruiters and hiring companies are: experience, impact, potential, stability, quality, presence, passion, influence, intelligence, and reputation.

)) By periodically re-taking the EPAM self-diagnostic assessment every few years, you will gain an appreciation for your standing in the job market at a given point in time and how your profile is developing. Importantly, you will be able to monitor where you can further enhance your EPAM score to grow an even stronger profile.

Notes:

5

STEP FIVE

Master the Building Blocks of Successful Career Management

"When I was young, I had to learn the fundamentals of basketball. You can have all the physical ability in the world, but you still have to know the fundamentals."

— *Michael Jordan*

। । । ।

Be like Mike! He was arguably the greatest professional basketball player of all time. You may have all the ability and potential in the world—intelligence, presence, desired skill sets, interpersonal abilities and ambition. However, if you are not aware of nor able to master the fundamentals of successful career management, you will not make the most of your potential. It's a terrible thing to waste in today's rich and dynamic professional environment.

There has never been a more exciting time to be an executive. The pace of change in businesses around the globe is unprecedented. New industry leaders are now built in 8 to 15 years, not 25 to 75 years. Product and service innovations are swift. Think about the smartphone capabilities we now carry in the palm of our hands every day. Yet, the original iPhone came to market only 10 years ago. The Internet has brought a previously unseen level of transparency, speed, and capabilities to reach, influence, sell, service and monitor market activity. As a result, a wide range of industry sectors and traditional business models—retail, financial services, insurance, travel, publishing, telecommunications, hospitality, entertainment, education, advertising, and healthcare, to name a few—have been disrupted. The corporate landscape has undergone a tremendous amount of disruption over the last 20 years due to globalization, technology innovation, quickly emerging competitors, political forces, and maturing markets here in the U.S.

This swiftly evolving business landscape carries with it a heightened need for effective, agile and proactive career management. The risks of not managing your career have never been greater. Unprepared and unwary executives may quickly find that their skill sets are obsolete, their role has been supplanted by a robo-advisor or artificial intelligence, or that their company's very existence is in question. The average tenure of today's executive with an employer is in the four- to five-year range. This means that in the span of a 40-year career, a professional may change jobs 8 to 10 times. Gone are the days when most executives worked for a company for fifteen or more years.

Preparation for the new and unexpected is now essential.

Today's executive needs an agile and proactive mindset to navigate both the opportunities and perils of today's corporate landscape. Preparation for the new and unexpected is now essential. Understanding and continually working to master the following skills will help you carve out a successful career path, which will most likely not be linear. Here are the fundamental building blocks of successful career management:

- Targeted Job Search Skills
- Effective Networking
- Continuous Resume Building
- Successful Interviewing
- Reference Cultivation
- Negotiation Skills
- Selectivity
- Transition Management

The following provides proven and practical insights and suggestions for each of these building blocks for effectively managing your career. They will help you make the right decisions, and take the right actions throughout your career:

Targeted Job Search Skills

Searching for a new job brings with it a range of emotions—exhilaration, hope, uncertainty, nervousness, and exhaustion. Searching for the right job requires the same amount of time and commitment that you bring to your professional role. You will need to be reflective, disciplined, organized, and very conscientious in your efforts and follow up throughout your search. If you never had to conduct a job search or not done so in a long time, the prospect of having to begin one can leave you feeling quite lost, especially if your early efforts are unsuccessful.

I recall one executive named John, who was referred to me for some one-on-one coaching. He was very well educated—with a J.D., M.B.A. and a C.P.A.—and had previously risen to Chief Operating Officer of a mid-sized digital media and content company over a 15-year span. When he initially started, there were less than 20 employees. He had grown the company to 1,000 full-time employees and almost as many contract employees across 25 countries. He had also significantly grown the company's revenue and profits. As a result, the business had attracted outside interest and was successfully sold to a private equity firm.

Following the transition to new ownership, John had departed the company. He had never had to look for a job, having always been sought after by others. Over a nine-month timeframe, John had aggressively networked, speaking with 270 people. His job search, however, was not producing any fruit. He was becoming concerned and frustrated. During my initial meeting with John, it quickly became apparent that his resume was not adequately showcasing his successes. Additionally, his job search was scattered and not well targeted. We put a plan in place that allowed

John to position and present his experience and skill sets with greater clarity and differentiation, bring this clarity into his interviews and personal presentation, and to have greater focus in his networking and selection of target companies of potential interest. John is presently working with an online ratings and reviews company as an operating-oriented Chief Financial Officer.

Job searches are typically the result of being terminated, resigning, or proactively seeking a more suitable job while you are still employed. How you approach your job search will vary somewhat based on each of these circumstances.

Mounting a Job Search after a Termination

Terminations can occur for many different reasons—a misfit with a role or organization culture, poor performance, centralization of job functions, downsizing, a new management team, industry consolidation, or a merger. Before you leave your position, you should fully understand your organization's severance policy and packages (if any), as well as whether it will provide you with job search assistance through an outplacement firm.

In many instances, you may have a sense that a potential termination is developing. In other cases, the signs may be more subtle. Perhaps you missed the signs because you were too busy focusing on your job, not attuned to internal dynamics, or misunderstood how secure your role was.

What are some of subtle signs of dissatisfaction with your performance or of an impending termination? Your superior suggests that you get some outside coaching. Colleagues seem more distant. There are meetings where your presence is not required. You are not copied on emails. Your boss seems less attentive and interested in what you are saying or doing. Your boss is going around you to talk directly with your team.

Whatever the reason, there's a lot to be learned from a job termination. So, when mounting an effective job search after a termination, you first need to understand why the termination occurred. Doing so offers a learning opportunity that will help you prevent future terminations for the same reason and help you recognize termination warning flags. Take some time—a few days or several weeks—to digest what has happened and consider what you might have done differently. Explore whether there are any job search support groups near you. Such groups offer networking, resources and discussions relevant to your job search. When you begin to start your job search after such reflection, you are more likely to seek opportunities that will be a better fit for you—perhaps a different job in the same industry, the same job in a different industry, or a less volatile industry or company, for example.

The good news about a termination is that it frees up all of your time to mount an open job search. An open and public job search has no constraints with regards to where you forward your resume and with whom you talk—other than companies mentioned in your non-compete clause, should you have one. Approach your job search as you would a full-time job. Before putting too much time and distance between you and your former employer, come to an understanding with your recent organization and superior about how they will talk about you, your performance, and your departure. Future employers will likely want to understand this. The best way to do this is have an open, direct and honest conversation with your prior superior and the references that you have been proactively cultivating within and outside the organization. Discuss specifically how your departure can be positioned in the least damaging manner. Be specific and reasonable with your suggestions. Provide both your superior and references with a resume or sheet of paper that reviews your contributions and accomplishments. Doing so will provide these individuals talking points consistent with how you would like to be represented.

When interviewing with potential employers or recruiters after a termination, you will want to communicate a story that is consistent with what you anticipate your prior superior and references will describe. This consistency provides credibility and diminishes reluctances that employers might have. If you were terminated for reasons outside of your control—downsizing, reorganizations, restructuring, a merger or acquisition, or new senior managers who want to bring in their own team—you should make sure that employers and recruiters understand this. They will recognize that sometimes unfortunate things occur to good people. If you have prior examples on your resume of longer term (more than four years of employment with other organizations), you will want to highlight this stability. If you have received promotions or taken on increased levels of responsibility within these prior companies, that is also worth noting. If your departure was due to a bad decision you made in joining your prior employer, it can be helpful to share what you learned in the process and what you will do differently in the future.

As you mount your job search, keep in mind that the more flexibility you have regarding geography, compensation, and the type and size of an organization, the greater the number of opportunities you will see and—in all likelihood—the quicker your job search will be. A job search can be a wonderful opportunity to explore roles or industries that you have not previously considered. Explore these opportunities with purpose and focus. Such opportunities should leverage your strengths and prior experience—in other words, have a strong common thread with your past. The clock is ticking, and you do not want to waste your time, energy and money pursuing options that do not make sense based on your goals or background. Opportunities should be assessed with an eye on how they would continue to build your resume and executive profile in a meaningful manner.

> A job search can be a wonderful opportunity to explore roles or industries that you have not previously considered.

Generally speaking, the more senior you are, the longer it is likely to take for you to identify and land the right opportunity. This is primarily because the more senior you are, the fewer roles exist. There is a point in time—perhaps 7 months or 9 months into your search—where others will wonder why you have not found a new job or have active irons in the fire. Employers will begin to wonder whether you are "damaged" goods. If your job search is not showing progress and some momentum at the 4 to 7 month mark, you will want to step back and determine what you need to do differently. At this point, you may want to obtain some objective advice from a career coach or recruiter.

If you happen to be terminated for cause, it means that you have shown a serious lack of judgement that your company views as grave misconduct. When an executive's employment is terminated for cause, the employment is terminated immediately for a reason which is given to the executive and stated in the termination letter. Examples of behaviors, actions, and misjudgments that lead to termination with cause either put other people or your company at risk—stealing company money or property, falsifying records, failing an alcohol or drug test, padding expense reports, sexual harassment, failure to follow company policy, insider trading, and threatening behavior, among many other reasons. In such circumstances, the executive typically loses any right to severance compensation, unpaid bonuses, and healthcare coverage, although situations vary according to the severity of the misbehavior.

Use your best judgement during the course of your career. Putting your livelihood, future, reputation and family at risk for such misbehavior is simply not something you should ever consider. Termination for cause becomes a permanent stain on your record. However, should you wittingly or unwittingly be terminated for cause, face the situation head-on, own up to your misbehavior, get counseling assistance if needed, and move on with your life as best you can. Others will find out about this misbehavior. These things never stay a secret. When asked in the future about this misbehavior, explain what a painful and poignant lesson you have learned and that you are ready to return to work in a responsible manner.

❯❯ Mounting a Job Search after a Resignation

People resign for one of two primary reasons: they are either unhappy in their present organization or role, or they have received what they view to be a better opportunity. In either of these situations, it is important that you leave gracefully and not burn bridges. If you have resigned or are planning to resign because of unhappiness in a role, explore whether there might be more suitable and interesting opportunities elsewhere in your present organization. If there are, this provides you with not only a new learning opportunity but signals to the external world that your organization values you and is making an effort to keep you on the team. If there are not any roles of interest, give proper notice, have appropriate conversations with your superior and colleagues you have worked closest with, tie up loose ends, transition your work, and keep your discussions positive.

I do not generally encourage a professional to leave an organization without having another job secured. In addition to not having a paycheck after your resignation, people will naturally assume that you were let go. Unfortunately, "job seekers" are not generally viewed as favorably as those who are "employed." The best time to look for a job is when you have a job. You are viewed more positively, do not feel as much pressure, and can take the time to be more selective in your job search. For whatever reasons, it seems that when an executive is unemployed, there are not as many interesting roles materializing as anticipated. It's kind of like police patrol cars...when you need one, they're not around. When you don't need one, they seem to be on every corner!

> **The best time to look for a job is when you have a job.**

What should you do if you have recently accepted a new job only to find that your decision was a mistake, or that a better job came along? If the mistake offers the opportunity to make some notable contributions, try staying with the role for a while. If not, cut your losses and be very considerate and respectful as you prepare to leave. In these cases, it is better to leave sooner rather than later. If you remain with the company for over a year and then decide to leave, there is a greater tendency for others to think that you were let go for various reasons—none good. When leaving, acknowledge that you did not properly do your homework or that you should have pushed harder for certain information. Do not lay blame on others. If your role or budget diminished significantly following your hiring, others outside the company will understand your disappointment. When leaving, bend over backwards to ensure a smooth transition. This quick move should be reflected on your resume. To not include the position and have this discovered can trigger questions about the veracity of your entire job history.

> When leaving, bend over backwards to ensure a smooth transition.

If you are resigning for a better opportunity offered by another employer, think very carefully about the implications of accepting the role. If you have been with your current employer only a short period of time, moving to a new role will appear to be a quick move on your resume. In the future, this may raise some questions about your loyalty, judgement or ability to contribute. Unless your absolute "dream job" is being offered, I counsel executives to stay with the initial role they accepted. Doing otherwise makes you look opportunistic and unreliable. The employer you initially joined is left with an urgent void, which can impact his or her business. Additionally, if the role you are leaving is the result of an executive search and you have been there less than one year, the retained search consultant who placed you in the job will need to re-do the search for no fees. In the search business, we call this a "do-over." Recruiters hate do-overs! So, you not only risk ruining your reputation with the initial employer, you also risk hurting your reputation with your search consultant and the executive search firm he or she represents. Notes about this will be entered into the corporate database that others across the search firm can see.

On the other hand, if you have been at your current employer for a minimum of three to four years or more and you are presented with an attractive outside opportunity…this is a different situation. Presuming that you decide to accept this opportunity, after weighing the pros and cons, you will want to make sure that you exit gracefully, giving proper notice, maintaining positive relationships, and showing appreciation for the experience and opportunity you have had at your current company.

I remember a conversation with a senior marketing executive, John. I was interested in considering him for a key marketing leadership role with a consumer-services client company. John was interested in the role and we both agreed that I would present his background to the hiring executive at our client. This hiring executive had worked in another company seven years prior where John also worked. When John abruptly left that earlier company with little notice to accept another role, his abrupt departure left the organization in a difficult spot. As a result of that occurrence, our client had formed the impression that John was an individual who was out for himself, and that he was unreliable. John had not shown consideration for how his actions impacted others. While our client thought John was skilled, he would not meet with him because of this past experience.

⟫ Mounting a Job Search While Employed

Seeking a new role outside of your current organization while you are still employed is an endeavor that needs to be conducted with confidentiality, discretion, and sensitivity. The last thing you want is for your boss or coworkers to hear that you are interviewing elsewhere. They will view this as disloyal, and may feel that you have already "checked out."

In these situations, you will want to keep tight control over the circulation of your resume and work with recruiters you trust and who understand how to deal with this level of confidentiality. Make certain that these parties fully appreciate that you are gainfully employed and do not want to jeopardize your role and good standing in your current organization. This discretion needs to be carried out through the full recruitment process—from initial overtures and declaration of interest, to interviews and references.

)) Mounting a Successful, Targeted Job Search

Regardless of the scenario that prompted your job search—termination, resignation or looking while employed—there are a number of key steps to every successful job search:

- **Know Your Goals and Parameters before You Start:** Understand what type of roles and organizations you are looking for and what you hope to achieve in taking a new role. Keep in mind that some flexibility in your job requirements is helpful. Determine your relocation parameters and a level of compensation that is both desirable and realistic. Determine the key job selection criteria against which you will measure the attractiveness of opportunities. Importantly, keep in mind how the next role fits into the long-term development of your executive profile.

- **Leverage Your Network:** Schedule a significant number of targeted informational discussions with your network. Talk with those who have recently mounted successful job searches. Learn how they went about their search. Ask for advice. Determine what worked and did not work from people you trust.

- **Prepare an Effective Resume and Cover Letter:** Have a concise resume that is ideally no more than two to two and a half pages long and which cites your accomplishments. (I will discuss resumes in more depth later in this chapter.) Cover letters accompanying your resume should be brief (a half page) and clarify the linkage between your background, interests and the specific opportunity. Some research into each position and company will allow you to make these connections effectively. Cover notes to search consultants should bullet point your geographic priorities, timing, types of opportunities and business sectors in which you are interested, as well as your compensation parameters. This information allows recruiters to more effectively target roles that meet your criteria and to not waste their time or yours.

■ **Look for a Good Fit:** These days, organizations tend to be quite specific about needs, experience requirements and skill sets in their position descriptions. Do not waste time chasing roles that are not a good fit for your background or future interests. Look for a strong fit between the role and your core strengths and experiences.

■ **Connect with Search Firms:** Contacting the right executive search firms, search consultants and research associates is important to gaining visibility in this community. Make certain that your preferred and most relevant executive search contacts have an updated resume and accurate information in their data bases. However, don't depend entirely on search firms to uncover opportunities for you. In general, only about 35% of job opportunities will come from search firms. This figure may be a bit higher or lower, depending on the specifics of your background and stage of your career. You will hear about opportunities through your network, friends and professional associates as well as through online postings and by contacting companies you have a particular interest in. You should also have a full profile on LinkedIn, which many internal corporate recruiting departments now access daily.

■ **Explore New Roles:** Do not be afraid to sensibly explore other industries, types of companies, and related job roles. As you do this, keep in mind that there should be a reasonably strong "common thread" to your experience and skill sets. Remember, you are always working toward the big picture and strategic enhancement of your executive profile. If there are opportunities that can help you prepare for the next level of your career, by all means use transitions to help you lay that foundation.

■ **Keep in Touch:** Once you've successfully completed your job search and moved into your new role, make sure to let others know of your whereabouts and new role. Provide updated contact information. This should include search firms so that they can update their databases. It is also a good idea to update your LinkedIn profile.

- **Mind Your Attitude:** Job searches are rarely over on the first job interview. They can be taxing and long. No matter what your job search throws at you, always maintain a positive, upbeat, enthusiastic attitude—even when you're frustrated. Additionally, and importantly, never bad mouth former employers or co-workers.

Every Job Transition Is an Opportunity for Self-Assessment

Beginning a job search is a golden opportunity to gain honest and objective feedback that will guide your ongoing professional development, provide valuable insights, and help you identify future roles that are a good fit. In an open job search, the most effective way to gain input is to have an executive coach or outplacement service conduct telephone references with prior superiors, peers and subordinates. Do this soon after you have left the company so that you are still fresh in their minds. When these discussions are approached as an opportunity for others to provide helpful advice and insight, they are more likely to provide productive and candid feedback. Below are a series of questions that I have found helpful in gaining valuable insights into executives:

- **What are your general thoughts about how [executive's name] was viewed in ABC, Inc.?** The purpose of this question is to obtain a top-of-mind summary and determine whether there are particular topics that need to be probed more deeply.

- **What adjectives come immediately to mind in describing [executive's name] and how he or she was viewed by his or her superior, peers, and subordinates?** The answer to this question helps form an impression of how an executive related to others across the entire organization. It also indicates whether the executive can build effective internal working relationships.

Additionally, this question provides insight into a professional's work and management style.

- **What would you identify as the 3 or 4 key strengths that set [executive's name] apart from his or her peers?** The input from this question is used to help the executive build a differentiated market position and direct him or her toward future roles that allow expanded use of key strengths.

- **What would you identify as [executive's name]'s most needed areas for improvement?** By triangulating this question across prior superiors, peers and subordinates, valuable developmental insights are gained, providing an opportunity for the candidate to consider and act upon.

- **Does [executive's name] have the capacity and potential to step up to the next level? If yes, what does he or she need to do? If not, why not?** The input from these questions provides a timely, real-world perspective that can help define job and career objectives as well as provide action steps for a candidate to move to the next level.

- **How much did [executive's name] develop during the timeframe that you worked with him or her?** The answer to this question will depend partly on how long the candidate worked with an organization. The question is designed to gain insight into the professional's developmental curve and ability to grow and evolve.

- **Did [executive's name] relate and manage better up, down, or across your organization? Why do you think this was**? Considered along with the responses to the second question about adjectives used by superiors, peers and subordinates, this question will help provide perspective on the nature of a candidate's internal working relationships.

- **Why—to the best of your knowledge—did [executive's name] leave?** The collective input from this question will allow the candidate and his or her executive coach to properly frame the recent departure as well as better understand what the "market" may hear about the event. This information gives the executive needed input to help manage and shape perceptions following a departure. The longer an executive has been out of his or her position, the more difficult it becomes to retroactively control and shape perceptions about his or her departure.

A gifted and experienced career coach will ask further questions in a deliberate manner to probe deeper into key areas. This information will then be aggregated into a candid and insightful report, and reviewed and discussed with the candidate. This exercise is extremely valuable. Executives should take advantage of such learning opportunities periodically as they progress in their careers.

Effective Networking

Simply stated, networking is the process of cultivating long-term relationships for the purposes of exchanging information, sharing job opportunities, and increasing your visibility. The most effective networking is accomplished by building and maintaining personal relationships (versus cyber-relationships) with influential and highly respected professionals who know others in your profession, industry, or related tangents. If you build a strong reputation and become someone who is desirable to know, your networking efforts will be easier. Effective networking is not a one-way street. When you have an opportunity to help someone in your network, you should extend yourself. This might mean providing an introduction, helping someone's son or daughter, commenting on a business project of mutual interest, or simply forwarding an interesting article. If you look for opportunities to assist those in your network, you will find them in abundance. If you select and build your network with professionals whom you like and respect, networking can become an enjoyable activity.

> Effective networking is not a one-way street.

- Well-networked individuals build their contact base every week. Personally, I believe every phone conversation and in-person interaction is an opportunity to build a relationship and make a personal impression. After learning about an individual's background and determining to what degree your interests are aligned, you can then decide how much effort to invest in building and maintaining a connection.

- Social media has become a powerful means of supplementing your networking efforts and maintaining connections. If you are not active on LinkedIn, Facebook or Twitter, you will want to consider building your social presence. LinkedIn alone has more than 450 million members. When you receive a LinkedIn notice that one of your connections has received a new job or been promoted, send them a short congratulatory note. They may not respond, but they will likely remember. While social media is an asset, there is no substitute for physically meeting someone, shaking hands, and looking him or her in the eye. Breakfast, lunch, or coffee offer great opportunities and can be confined to a reasonable amount of time, if properly scheduled. People help and do business with those whom they know and like.

- It is important to maintain a contact list with essential information about the important and potentially most helpful people in your growing network. This can be done by creating a spreadsheet of contacts that lists name, title, company, dates contacted, what was discussed, helpful information provided, and timing of any required follow-up. You can then set calendar reminders in your smartphone or laptop. If you are not organized in your networking, you will quickly lose track. Additionally, having this information centralized provides an easy way to monitor your progress.

- If you're new to networking, there are a number of familiar places where you can start building relationships. Turn first to former and current colleagues, school friends, alumni gatherings, association meetings and conferences, church, professional groups, professional training programs, and industry conferences. If you have the mindset that every professional interaction is a networking opportunity, the possibilities become endless. However, be mindful that your networking continues to be targeted and purposeful.

■ Industry conferences provide unique opportunities to build key relationships. Schedule multiple, short, one-on-one meetings before and during conferences. I personally have had great success in these venues, and schedule as many as 15 to 20 half-hour meetings in a two-day conference while having another 15 to 20 unplanned but noteworthy conversations with others at events surrounding the conference.

)) The Power of Convening

When we were building Spencer Stuart's Internet Practice in the late 1990s, we hit an unusual roadblock that turned into an excellent networking opportunity. It became apparent in our early executive search work for Internet CEOs and senior executives that this group had their heads down 24 hours a day, 7 days a week. Because of this, we were challenged to get their attention. While they were busy forming their companies, securing funding, hiring executives and managing rapid growth, the one thing they weren't doing was talking with each other.

Working with one Internet leader, Steve—who was a prior client and later became affiliated with Groupon—I proposed gathering (i.e., convening) a select group of 20 Internet leaders at his company headquarters for dinner. The purpose was to provide a venue for off-record conversations about the attendees' challenges. Steve was pleased to host the event (cocktail reception and dinner) and in the process show off his office space. We sent out invitations for what later became known as the Digital Leadership Exchange (DLX). The event was an immediate success and a great experience for the participants, many of whom had never met each other before.

The appetite for further DLX events was expansive. Through word of mouth, we were soon receiving requests for invitations to future DLX gatherings from other Internet leaders. The fact that we kept attendance limited to 20-25 executives made the event even more desirable. They were chasing us, we were no longer chasing them! Each event was themed around a specific topic of interest to the group which built their knowledge base and ours. Based on our early success, we approached Google's Chicago office to co-sponsor these gatherings with Spencer Stuart. Google offered to host the future receptions and dinners in its innovative tech space. The continued co-branding of this event between two respected industry leaders (Google and Spencer Stuart) was highly compelling. The positioning of Spencer Stuart with Google was powerful and further built our image and credibility in the Internet space. Google, in turn, was introduced to many senior executives.

In the years that followed, we went on to host repeat events in eight cities around the globe. In the process, members of our local offices—including myself—expanded our networks, generated awareness and built credibility for Spencer Stuart's Internet Practice. Over time, we became recognized leaders in this market sector. Convening talented people is a flexible and powerful form of networking. It can be done at any level with peers of similar interests. Try it!

Continuous Resume Building

During the course of my many years in executive search, I screened upwards of 100,000 resumes. I have seen pretty much every form of resume on the planet. Many of these resumes I've reviewed were "OK" but not as compelling as they could have been. There is a significant difference and impact between a good resume and a great one.

Your resume is the embodiment of who you are as a professional. It is both the story of your professional development and a marketing document. It should be attractively formatted, organized, easy to read, honest, articulate and compelling. The best resumes provide succinct contextual understanding of where you have worked and what you have done. For example, if a company or role on your resume is not well recognized, it should be accompanied with a brief description. Throughout your career, you should remain attentive to your end goals and the big picture as you build and shape your resume. In other words, your career decisions and experiences should be moving you closer to your career objectives and positioning you attractively in the market. If you are on a positive professional trajectory, is that story being effectively told on your resume? Here are my suggestions for crafting a compelling resume:

- If you are early in your career, a one-page resume is usually sufficient. By mid-career, a page and a half suffices. If you are advanced in your career, you can go to two pages or maybe even two and a half. In my experience, a one-page resume is not sufficient to tell the story of a tenured, experienced executive.

- I've mentioned this before, but it is worth repeating—on your resume, do not omit employers. Do not mislead about your educational credentials. Do not exaggerate your accomplishments, titles or the roles you have held. Integrity is crucial. If you are discovered to be misleading people with even one item on your resume, the veracity of the remainder of your resume will come into question. A less than forthcoming approach will tarnish your reputation and credibility and potentially eliminate you from further consideration for present and perhaps future opportunities.

- Your resume's format should be easy on the eyes. If it is text heavy, dense, and offers limited white space, the reader's first impression might be negative. If the reader must labor through a lot of detail, he or she might think you lack the ability to be succinct. As a result, your profile might receive only a perfunctory read. You need to be able to hold the reader's attention and draw the reader in.

- List your experience in reverse chronological order, with your most recent job first. Make dates, companies and locations clear and scannable.

- The most effective resumes share a greater amount of information about the most recent positions held and less about earlier ones. Do not omit any positions you have held. Each plays a role in showing the progression and breadth of your career. Descriptions of more recent roles should provide detail such as key responsibilities; size of the responsibility in terms of revenue, budget, headcount; to whom you reported; and (if applicable) what functions/titles reported to you.

- Bullet meaningful accomplishments using action-oriented verbs and quantifiable measurement of results. The more recent the role, the more accomplishments you may list. Generally, four to five bullets is sufficient for current or recent roles. Similarly, the more time you spent in a role, the greater the number of accomplishments you might list. Be sensitive about how far back in your job history the accomplishments occurred. I often see resumes that are structured entirely in bullet point format for both job responsibilities and accomplishments. In such a structure, the achievements become lost in a sea of bullet points. Reserve bullet points for key accomplishments so that they will stand out on your resume. You can also draw greater attention to your accomplishment in each position with an underlined or bold subtitle preceding the bullets such as, "Key Accomplishments."

- It's not a bad idea to include an "Executive Summary" at the top of your resume. It should be brief (4-6 sentences) and supportable. If done properly, an executive summary serves as an invitation into the rest of the resume. Think of it as your "elevator pitch." You may also want to add an "Objectives" section, describing the type of role you are seeking. If you are too specific in the objectives statement, however, it might prove limiting.

- I am not a big fan of some outplacement resume formats. They are often formatted to hide inadequacies and shortcomings or call attention away from a candidate's many job moves. The truth ultimately comes out. Some of these formats take the better half of the first page to describe a candidate's positive points before actually citing job history or experience. It's the chronological history of your experience and track record that most recruiters and employers want to see first.

■ Compensation information should not be a part of your resume. Neither should references or an undue amount of personal information. If you want to briefly list several hobbies or interests, you can do so. It is also fine to list professional affiliations, awards and recognitions, if they are relevant or meaningful. If you graduated with a strong grade point average or honors, that's okay to share as well. For privacy, you may want to list only the town that you reside in versus your full home address. Do, however, include your phone number and preferred email address.

On the following several pages, I have provided two examples of resumes. The first is an original resume that did not receive significant interest in the market. The second is the reworked version of that same resume, which garnered significant interest. The name of the executive and names of the companies have been changed to preserve anonymity of the individual.

You'll notice that the second resume provides the following:

■ Greater context

■ A more compelling story

■ More white space

■ A crisply written, attention-getting "executive summary"

■ Bullet points that highlight key accomplishments, not job duties.

(Example of Less Effectively Structured Resume)

JOHN SMITH
Austin, TX
512-999-9999 jsmith@mail.com

SUMMARY
- Senior level executive with extensive experience in management, strategic management, operations, financial, and legal.
- Proven record of accomplishment of growth plan execution culminating in significant increases in enterprise value.
- Extensive background in global mergers and acquisitions including planning and executing strategy, acquisition negotiation, integration, and on-going operation of new entities.
- Successful performance managing global operating budgets.
- Responsible for contract deliverables and client relationships for many major clients including Microsoft, Apple, Google, Yahoo, among many others.
- Execution-focused leader with a proven track record of developing people and processes in multicultural environments to deliver results.
- Effective leadership skills managing a global organization.

EXPERIENCE
DIGICORP LLC Austin, TX..2000 – 2016
DIGICORP is a digital content and media company that pioneered advanced capture distribution technology for photographs and graphic representations.

Chief Operating Officer 2013 – 2016

Executive Vice President 2005 – 2013

Sr. Vice Presiden 2000 – 2005
- Directed operations and staff of company under three different ownership structures.
- Managed growth from 30 employees to approximately 1,000 plus an additional 500 contract photographers.
- Increased revenue 40X — representing a 35% average annual increase.
- Increased sales to a world-wide client roster from a solely domestic reach.
- Expanded coverage 6X to cover content relevant in all regions of the world.
- Controlled expenses through creation of global operating standards and staffing ratios while ensuring quality, resulting in the ability to shift significant workload to lower cost regions.
- Sale of company to Rollup Equity Partners at a significant premium.
- Directed global operations consisting of:
  - Data collection / content creation from 20 collection centers/ 500 employees and stringers world-wide covering +200,000 events annually.
  - Aggregating to 10,000,000 photographs annually.
  - Complete research and analysis for publisher support including digital downloads.
  - Software development and maintenance for all collection tools and monitors across all product activities.
  - Technical customer service in all languages 24/7 with aid of internal system / workflow monitors and dashboards coupled with an extensive on-call system.

- IT / Systems coverage on a 24/7 basis including complete disaster recovery and contingency plans.
- Contract administration and client satisfaction through client liaison staff in all regions
- Responsible for client delivery 24/7 including the standardization of client offerings across all regions.
- Led 12 M&A and four joint ventures including negotiation, due diligence, closing and integration.
- Analysis of strategic direction and consideration of alternative growth strategy for presentation to BOD for approval.
- Led four international market expansions and stabilized operations ahead of schedule leading to outperformance of budgets.
- Executive team included: Operations Director – oversight of collection and customer satisfaction in all offices; Head of IT / Systems – oversight of product management, development, and engineering; financial oversight including CFO / Interim CFO / head of finance, CFO oversight.
- Acted as Corporate BOD secretary and counsel and member BOD for all subsidiaries; General counsel / interim general counsel including litigation oversight, general legal strategies, and complete client contract process.
- Served as secretary and counsel for Board of Directors meetings. Member of Board of Directors for several subsidiaries and JV's.
- Oversaw international activities including International Head of HR, finance, administration, legal and sales for all international offices.
- Implemented global operating and performance standards and MBOs for operations staff.
- Positioned company for sale including management presentations to prospective buyers, due diligence, and closing.
- Creation of global software and hardware infrastructure platform and migration to new systems.
- Transformation from a data company to a global products and technology and services enterprise.

SENIOR LIVING CORPORATION Dallas, TX
Vice President of Development ....1998 – 2000
Senior Living Corporation owns and operates a variety of senior living projects, including assisted and independent living, memory care, and skilled nursing. A joint venture with MMM Capital. Senior Living is now privately owned and operated.

- Managed strategic growth through new projects in the greater Houston area.

SOUTH LIVING COMPANY Atlanta, GA
President — SLC Development Corp ....1993 – 1998
Vice President — SLC Venture Fund
SOUTH LIVING is the development office of several ownership groups of skilled nursing and assisted living facilities.

- Managed strategic growth through new development including the regulatory/license approval, design, construction, finance, and operation.
- SOUTH LIVING Venture Fund is a portfolio of investment assets managed for the various Principals outside of the core company mission.
- Managed the portfolio of assets.

CATTLEMAN BANK NA Houston, TX
Vice President — Commercial Loans Division ....**1991 – 1993**
Cattleman Bank is a holding company for a group of Houston-based banks.
Managed portfolio of loan workouts and turnarounds of the underlying assets.
A member of the workout and turnaround team handling troubled loans and
owned assets. Reduced the holding companies' exposure to troubled loans
ahead of schedule and shifted activities to commercial lending.

THE SCHWINDLER GROUP Amarillo, TX
Assistant Vice President—Project Development and Acquisitions **1990– 1991**
A real estate partnership focused on industrial and office assets (now Second
Industrial REIT). Worked on project finance and strategic development of new
opportunities in the industrial market.

FRANKLIN FINANCIAL Dallas, TX
Loan Analyst — Commercial Real Estate Lending ....**1988 – 1990**
Franklin Financial was a credit company lender focused on asset based lending.
Worked as a credit analyst on the various loans presented for approval.

SMITH HORTON
Senior Accountant — Audit Division ....**1985 – 1987**
Brant Thornton provides audit, tax, and advisory services.

CERTIFICATION
Admission to the Bar of the State of Texas 1995
Certified Public Accountant, State of Texas 1987

EDUCATION
University of Texas, JD 1997
University of Illinois, MBA 1987
Indiana University — Kelley School of Business, BS 1984

(Example of Well-Structured Resume)

JOHN SMITH CPA, JD, MBA
Austin, TX
512-999-9999 jsmith@mail.com

EXECUTIVE SUMMARY
Results and growth oriented digital media/content/information services COO/CFO with broad ranged operating responsibilities across all key business functions except marketing. Have overseen complex global operations spanning 600 full time employees plus 750 contract employees across 25 countries. Successfully grew recent company to market leader and positioned the company for successful sale to private equity, staying on for another two years.

EXPERIENCE

DIGICORP LLC...**2000 – 2016**
Austin, TX
A private equity-backed company, DigiCorp is a $100 million market leading provider of digital media. The company is best known for its patented photographic information capture technology. The company possesses one of the world's largest databases of photographic images servicing customers worldwide such as Google, Microsoft, Yahoo, Verizon, CBS and Fox.

Chief Operating Officer (2013 – 2016)
Reporting to the CEO as Co-COO from 2013–2014 and as COO from 2014–2016, oversaw all operations across North America and 25 countries. Solid line reports included: Directors for IT, Finance (Controller, Bank Relationships/line of credit), Administration, Research, Product, Engineering/Software Development and Maintenance, Customer Service, Content Development, Legal, M&A, Strategic Planning and International Sales, plus SVPs of Client Delivery and Broadcast Research and Support. Also directly oversaw activities of Managing Directors in 25 countries across Europe, Latin America, Middle East, and Asia.

The complexity of the business was significant with content creation from 20 collection centers and 500 employees plus 700 contract photographers worldwide covering +200,000 events aggregating 10,000,000 photographs annually. Customer service was 24/7 in all necessary languages.

Key accomplishments:
- Provided critical operational leadership in growing a domestic company from $15 million in revenue and 30 employees in 2000, to $100 million (+35% annually) and 1,000 employees plus 500 contract employees in 2016. Sold company to private equity buyer at a significant premium.
- Led four international market expansions and stabilized operations ahead of schedule leading to outperformance of budgets.
- Led 12 M&A and 4 joint ventures, including negotiation, due diligence, closing and integration.
- Implemented global operating and performance standards and MBOs for operations staff, enabling exceptional customer service, product, and geographic expansion in a highly cost-effective manner.

Executive Vice President (2005 – 2013)
Reporting to the CEO, oversaw the integration of the newly merged entity, international expansion into Europe and Asia and the integration of the newly acquired technology. Solid line reports included Directors for IT, Research, Product, Engineering/Software Development, and Maintenance, Customer Service, Finance, Legal, International Sales, Content Development, M&A, Strategic Planning and International Sales, plus VPs of Client Delivery and Support.

Key accomplishments:
- Transformation of company via merger/joint venture with a division of the Associated Photographics creating a powerhouse offering of best-in-class content capture and advanced search capabilities based on word and visual query integration.
- Created and executed strategy of global expansion into Europe and Asia through a mix of M&A and joint ventures and creation of new markets.
- Achieved revenue growth of 2.9X and EBITDA growth of 2.2X through creation of new market segments and technology enhancements. This growth involved expansion of employee base by 300%.
- Acquired technology start-up in India for non-invasive tracking of objects through image processing and expanded application for global publishers and media companies, as well as the creation of a development center in Bangalore.

Sr. Vice President (2000 – 2005)
Reporting to the President until 2003 and then the CEO, oversaw the Content Licensing Division and then took on further responsibility for all customer delivery, customer service, and content development. Solid line reports included Directors for Content Collection and Licensing, Customer Service and Legal.

Key accomplishments:
- Restructured largest revenue unit to streamline and enhance customer delivery experience; created 24x7 customer service function.
- Directed operations and instituted standard operating procedures and service upgrades to obtain efficiency and position for growth.
- Coordinated software upgrades and enhancements for location agnostic content collection and entry providing a level of increased quality.

SENIOR LIVING CORPORATION..**1998 – 2000**
Dallas, IL
Senior Living Corporation owns and operates a variety of senior living projects, including assisted and independent living, memory care, and skilled nursing. Through a joint venture with MMM Capital, Senior Living is now privately owned and operated.

Vice President of Development
Responsibilities included strategic growth through new projects—identification, financing, construction, and opening.

SOUTHERN LIVING COMPANY..**1993 – 1998**
Atlanta, GA
SLC Development Corp is the development office of several ownership groups of skilled nursing and assisted living facilities charged with expansion through new projects from project identification through regulatory/ license approval, design, construction, and finance.

President — SLC Development Corp
(Held concurrently with VP – SLC Venture Fund role below) SLC Venture Fund is a portfolio of investment assets managed for the various SLC principals outside of the core company mission.

Vice President — SLC Venture Fund
Responsibilities included management of the portfolio investments.

CATTLEMAN BANK NA...**1991 – 1993**
Houston, TX
Cattleman Bank NA is a holding company for a group of Houston-based banks.

Vice President – Commercial Loans Division
Managed portfolio of loan workouts and turnarounds of the underlying assets.

THE SHWINDLER GROUP...**1990 – 1991**
Amarillo, TX
Assistant Vice President — Project Development/Acquisitions

FRANKLIN FINANCIAL ....**1988 – 1990**
Dallas, TX
Loan Analyst — Commercial Real Estate Lending

SMITTH HORTON ....**1985 – 1987**
Senior Accountant — Audit Division

****

CERTIFICATIONS
Admission to the Bar of the State of Texas 1995
Certified Public Accountant, State of Texas 1987

EDUCATION
College of Law — University of Texas, JD 1997
University of Illinois, MBA 1987
Indiana University – Kelley School of Business, BS 1984

Note that in the improved resume (pages 113–115), further company and position context have been added to enrich John Smith's story. The accomplishments have been highlighted so that they attract the recruiter's attention. The complexity and breadth of the candidate's responsibilities have been amplified.

Successful Interviewing

Congratulations! Your resume has caught a potential employer's attention. However, regardless of the strength of your professional track record or educational background, "hire" or "not to hire" decisions are based on how you come across during the interview process. If the interviews do not go well, it really doesn't matter how strong and well qualified a candidate you are. You are not likely to get hired and second chances are rare.

Interviews are a contrived and unique human interaction. Talking about your strengths, skills, prior positions, accomplishments, promotions, and job transitions in a one-hour interview can be daunting. In what other aspect of life are you expected to do something so structured and comprehensive in order to establish human connection? Maybe speed dating? There are obvious limitations as to how much can be conveyed in an interview. Therefore, your challenge is to communicate the information that is of the highest interest and value to the interviewer.

> There are obvious limitations as to how much can be conveyed in an interview.

"What are the key things companies look for in interviews?" This is a question I was asked often by candidates during my years in executive search. Here are my "Top 10" selection criteria that clients look for in an interview as well as thoughts about the type of insights employers and recruiters are seeking around each qualifying criteria:

1. Position Fit. Does this person have the experience and ﹖
to do the job well?

2. Leadership Abilities. Will this person embrace the challenge, create a "success" plan, and excite the organization to execute? Will they (he or she) identify and take advantage of meaningful opportunities? Are they able to form a team, harness resources, and motivate others? How much oversight do they need?

3. Intelligence and Learning Agility. Will this candidate understand the complexities of our organization and industry? When they don't know something, will they be able to figure it out? Does this person have the intelligence and/or "street smarts" to lead or advance in our organization over the long term?

4. Results. Will this candidate accomplish what I am bringing them in to do? Are they able to engender the support and cooperation of others? Will they remain focused on objectives and deliverables and accomplish them in a timely manner? Will they overcome obstacles? Do they have the desire and energy to go the extra mile in order to make things happen?

5. Team Player. Will this candidate be part of my team or a lone ranger? Can they work with and get along with others who are important to the operation? Is this an individual who we can rely on? Does this candidate readily provide credit to and develop others? Is this someone who will listen and receive input, ideas and suggestions from others?

6. Chemistry. Is this candidate someone with whom we can feel comfortable? Would we enjoy working with this person on a day-to-day basis? Is this someone we can communicate with easily and effectively? Do we have something in common with this potential employee?

7. Cultural Fit. Does this candidate relate to and embrace the style of how we do business? Do they share many of the same core values that have helped make us successful?

8. Potential. Does this candidate have the wherewithal to take on a larger role in our organization? How readily do they learn and adapt? Do they exhibit intellectual curiosity and inquisitiveness? Are they nimble and able to pivot when necessary? Can they continue to help us increase the value of what we are doing?

9. Interest. Does this professional really want to work with us, or are they merely out job interviewing? Are they asking insightful questions or going through the motions? Have they done their homework?

10. Value. Based on what we know about this candidate and others we have seen, do we believe their compensation requirements are in line with what we have to offer? Does this candidate offer a good and fair value relative to their compensation and what we believe this role should pay?

)) How to Make a Strong, Positive and Lasting Impression during a Job Interview

- You typically have at most 45 minutes to an hour to convey the many attributes listed above. Most interviewers will form an early impression in the initial five minutes, so when addressing questions be succinct and honest. Highlight convincing examples and successes. Be specific and provide tangible results— for example, explain how you contributed to an increase in the company or division's revenue and profit, expanded market share, or improved customer retention. Whenever possible, quantify these results.

- Communicate in a conversational tone and carry on a dialogue, not monologue. Don't monopolize the "air" space. If your ability to listen comes into question, the interviewer will inevitably ask themselves whether you are able to take others' points of view into consideration, whether you are a team player. The best interviews are those characterized by a dynamic interchange and volley of ideas, questions and active thoughts about the role or business. Through this interchange "chemistry" is developed. You want to come across as having genuine and well-founded enthusiasm.

- Managers hire those with whom they connect and with whom they would like to work. Though you want to be well prepared, you want to be genuine and authentic—not overly rehearsed.

- Today's flatter and more interconnected organization structures require collaboration, awareness, agility, and responsiveness. Take the opportunity to exhibit these attributes during interviews.

- When asked a question about how you can help address a potential employer's challenges, never paint yourself into a corner by sounding like you have all the answers. Instead, position your thoughts as a first impression based on your preliminary understanding of the company's business and situation. Follow-up questions can start a dialogue to showcase collaboration, intelligence and perceptiveness.

- By doing your homework before the interview, you will be better prepared to convey the right information in a compelling manner. Study the organization's business—its revenue model, performance, product lines, services, and competitors. If possible, review its annual report. Listen to an earnings call about the company. Look at its stock performance in the last one, three and five years. Check LinkedIn for the profiles of individuals you are meeting and see whether you have any common connections. Visit Glassdoor.com to see what others are saying about the company. Take a look at the company's ratings and reviews, if relevant.

- If possible and appropriate, talk with people who are currently employed with the company or have worked there in the past. Talk to some of the company's customers. Ask them about the reputation, culture, challenges and needs of the organization you are interviewing with. This "insider" perspective will help you create a dynamic and personal interchange of sharing information, thoughts, and observations. However, if an opportunity or executive search is confidential, be sure to protect the employer's confidentiality. Breeching such a confidence will eliminate you from further consideration, and might even have further repercussions.

- Ask in advance about the dress code for the interview. The objective is to look sharp but fit in with the company's culture and work style.

- Come prepared with a great set of questions to ask the interviewer. Otherwise, you have missed an opportunity to show your enthusiasm and gain further insight. Importantly, listen to the answers that you receive and ask follow-up questions. Probe more deeply whenever possible. If you have no questions, the interviewer will assume that you have not really thought seriously about the role. They may also come away with the impression that you are not probing or inquisitive by nature.

- Tailor your answers to the interview format and interviewer. Not all interviewers are created equal. Occasionally, interviewers will want to do most of the talking. In this instance, the best you can do is to try and interject relevant points about your background in a polite manner. A good way to conclude this type of interview is to ask the interviewer, "Is there anything else you would like to know about my background?" Typically, when I debrief talkative corporate clients, they comment, "I thought the interview went great!" That's okay.

›› Types of Interviews

Interviewers generally will have a preferred method of interviewing. Try to recognize an interviewer's style early on in the conversation. There are two types of interviews: unstructured interviews and competency-based or behavior-based interviews.

Unstructured interviews are conversational. Typically, the interviewer asks a few questions that are focused on understanding your resume and background. They are seeking an overall impression

of you as an individual and what you would bring to the r\
Questions are meant to gather basic information, not assess specific skills, competencies and behaviors. Unstructured interviews
are also referred to as informational interviews. Here are some
examples of unstructured interview questions that you can expect
to encounter, as well as some suggestions for responding:

- **Walk me through your background and explain your moves between companies and the reasons behind them.** The important thing to remember in answering open-ended questions like
this is to be succinct. Do not take more than 5-10 minutes to
answer such questions. You and the interviewer have lots to
talk about in the allotted 45-60 minutes for a typical interview
session, maybe less if the interview is a phone screen.

- **Tell me about the major influences that have shaped you both personally and professionally.** Here, again, be succinct.
The interviewer is looking to understand what has formed
and shaped the person sitting in front of him or her. Much
can be learned about a person's motivations and formation
by understanding the individual's earlier circumstances and
background.

- **What adjectives would individuals you have worked closely with use to describe you?** This is a favorite interview question
of mine. The answers to this question provide me a quick snap-
shot of how others perceive the candidate—who they are, their
reputation, and style. Phrasing this question in the context of
"others you have worked with" implies that I will want to verify this snapshot during future referencing.

- **If I were to speak with two of your most recent bosses (or peers or subordinates), what would they say about you?** This
is another favorite question of mine. It provides a glimpse of
how the interviewee believes he or she is viewed by others
throughout the firm and how consistent or different the perceptions are. During the referencing process, I will assess the
accuracy of the interviewee's initial responses.

- **What is it about your background that makes you a particularly strong and unique fit for this role?** This is an obvious question that you should expect and be prepared to answer concisely and with insight. A clear and compelling response will show both your understanding of the role and the quality of your candidacy.

- **What is it that interests you about this position and company?** With this question, the interviewer is seeking to understand the level of passion and commitment you would bring to the role and why you believe his or her company is special.

- **What would those with whom you've worked closely say are your greatest strengths? What would they say are your greatest areas of opportunity for improvement?** Questions such as these provide the interviewer with a sense of your self-awareness and understanding of personal strengths and shortcomings. Answers should be authentic without raising red flags. One approach is to acknowledge job requirements where you would need to supplement your learning or team. Your answers here will be further validated or invalidated at the referencing stage of the hiring process.

- **What questions about our company or the position do you have for me?** Don't be caught flat-footed. Have thoughtful questions prepared for the interviewer. If you are not prepared, you will come across as having limited interest or understanding about the role and company. Have a list of 5-10 thoughtful and insightful questions ready for this interview question.

Competency or behavior-based interviews focus on specific areas of knowledge, skills and how you do things—your behaviors. The interview is focused around a set of specific competencies required for a given position and how you have exhibited those competencies in actual workday scenarios. For a senior manager, the interviewer's competency assessment might include your ability to influence and negotiate, manage conflict, cope with stress and pressure, lead and inspire, or take calculated risks. Other examples of competencies would include delegation, adaptability, flexibility, awareness, resilience/tenacity, and teamwork. Behavior-based interviews are also referred to as structured interviews versus unstructured or informational interviews.

Some examples of competency/behavioral-based questions are:

- Provide an example of a situation where you had to resolve conflict with an internal or external client or customer.

- How do you influence people in situations where there are conflicting agendas?

- Tell me about the biggest change that you have had to deal with in your recent role. How did you cope with it?

- Tell me about a situation where your communication skills made a difference in a situation.

- Describe a situation where you had to deal with an angry customer.

- What big decision did you make recently? How did you go about it?

Preparation is key if you want to be able to answer competency-based questions without having to think too much on the spot. Make sure you understand which skills and competencies are required in the role for which you are interviewing. Many job specifications list these.

Identify examples from your past experience demonstrating that you possess the skills and competencies required for the position. You do not have to necessarily cite extraordinary examples. What matters most is the role you played and the outcome.

I suggest using the STAR (Scene, Task, Action, and Result) method of responding to these types of interview questions. This means setting the scene, explaining the task or problem, citing the actions you took to handle the situation, and detailing the outcome or result of your actions.

As a final suggestion, be sure to send a short, thoughtful follow-up note or email that is tailored to each interviewer, remarking on a point that he or she raised, and noting that you appreciated his or her time and the opportunity to learn more about the role and the organization. Reinforce your enthusiasm and belief that you could add value to his or her efforts. This note should be succinct and no more than two short paragraphs. If you are long-winded, you will do yourself a disservice. Also, do not be overly familiar in tone.

Reference Cultivation

Things are looking good! You've gone through several rounds of interviews and been selected as one of the top candidates under consideration for hire. The potential employer has asked for your references. Are you ready? The following provides suggestions for successfully navigating the referencing process:

- Proactively cultivate references from previous positions on an ongoing basis, long before you need them—include references from superiors, peers, subordinates and customers. Keep these individuals aware of your career activity.

- Think about who will be the most appropriate references for each role you are considering. Make sure to get permission early in the interview process to use them as a reference, if needed. Also, ensure that they are comfortable and enthusiastic about serving as a reference for you. Most people will be flattered—or at least willing to serve as a reference—but you still need to ask to be sure.

- Collect and organize all the details for each reference: the individual's name, current title and company and his or her title and the name of the company where you worked together. Potential employers will also request their contact information (phone and email), the nature of your prior relationship (superior, peer, or subordinate) and the years that you worked together.

- If your discussions and the role are not of a confidential nature, keep your references informed and perhaps even discuss the opportunity with them. This will provide some context for what they say about you. Ask your references whether they would find it helpful if you sent them a copy of your updated resume and the position description for the role you are being considered for.

■ If the discussions or potential job are confidential, you will want to select references who you believe will be able to uphold this required confidentiality. You may want to share some general information about the nature of the role with them. Do not, however, forward or email them information that might be considered sensitive. If you are gainfully employed, communicate clearly to the hiring organization and to your references that discussions should be treated confidentially.

■ Ask your references to send you a quick email when they have heard from the potential employer or recruiter. Be aware that some organizations check only one or two references while others will want to speak with five or more. Still others will seek the names of further references from the contacts that you have provided or reach out to folks they may know in your last organization through LinkedIn or otherwise. There is wide variation in how the reference process is conducted across hiring organizations. You can count on professional recruiting firms to be very thorough, given that their reputations are on the line.

■ As a common courtesy, thank your references once your current job search is complete and let them know your whereabouts.

■ Don't burn bridges with former employers. When you depart an organization, leave gracefully and with class. A poorly handled departure is not the final impression you want to leave. Memories are long and negative last impressions can color future references and your reputation.

■ An executive coach or outplacement service can help you pre-test your references. If someone you have chosen as a reference is not effective, an executive coach can help you navigate the problem early in the job search process. A weak reference can be a big detriment, but even the difference between a good reference and an exceptional one can be pivotal in your job search.

The following provides one example of a "good" reference for an executive named Sally versus another reference that is "exceptional." Notice how easily you are able to distinguish between the two.

Reference One: "Yes, I worked with Sally at ABC organization for 4 years. We interfaced weekly to monthly. She is a good person and worked very hard. Sally was pleasant and respectful of others. She did her job well and I believe she may have been promoted, although don't quote me on that. Her skill sets fit the role she was in. She was reliable and trusted. Tactically, she is capable. I never quite got a glimpse into her strategic thinking. She has potential."

Reference Two: "I very clearly recall working with Sally at ABC organization. We worked together for four years. We spent a fair amount of time together on a weekly to monthly basis—enough time that I understood why she was so broadly respected across the organization. She is very smart and capable. She brings an abundance of energy to the office and is such a pleasure to work with. Sally makes those around her better. She gives others credit and knows how to motivate her team. She is very proactive and anticipates potential issues before they arise. Sally is able to go deep into the detail or step back and take an insightful strategic perspective. Her recent promotion was well deserved. She has lots of potential, is a quick study, and is willing to be coached. If I were hiring right now, she would be someone I'd love to have on my team!"

Negotiation Skills

Congratulations, you are going to receive an offer! Do you feel good about this? You should not accept a new role primarily because it offers a higher level of compensation. That is short-sighted. There are significant non-compensation factors that should be considered—the quality of the organization, greater responsibilities and challenges, good cultural fit, personal growth prospects, and a boss for whom you are excited to work. If most of these factors are favorable, then and only then is it time to talk money.

You will likely already have an idea of what the role pays or what similar jobs in the industry pay. More often than not, you will have provided your compensation information to the company's internal recruiter, human resources department, or executive search consultant. This information should include your prior and current job's base salary, actual annual bonuses received (and an indication of whether the bonus payout was at target, above target, or below target), annual long-term incentive plan payouts (and whether they are cash or equity based, and how the payouts are structured and timed), and any meaningful perquisites (car, club membership, etc.). The potential employer or executive recruiters may ask you to verify these figures by providing a year-end pay stub or W-2. Be honest and accurate with the initial figures that you provide, so that everything matches up. Early in your career, pay and benefit discussions should be fairly straightforward. They will likely consist of a base salary, a bonus provided the company meets or exceeds performance targets, and medical insurance coverage. You should also ask about the company's vacation policy, if that information is not offered. As you progress in your career, long-term incentive plans (LTIPs) whether equity or cash based, will become a larger part of the discussion and a significant portion of your total compensation.

When negotiating compensation, there is a significant distinction between whether you are the pursuer or the pursued. If you are unemployed and without a paycheck, you may well be asked to make a lateral move in terms of compensation. You generally have less compensation leverage when unemployed. However, this can depend on the circumstances under which you've become unemployed and how those circumstances are

> You generally have less compensation leverage when unemployed.

viewed. Provided you are gainfully and happily employed, you may find yourself being pursued as opposed to being the pursuer. If this is the case, you have a stronger bargaining position. You don't need a new job. Thus, it is in the employer's interest to offer you a higher level of compensation to induce you to move. How much more depends on how unique your skills and experience are and whether there is relocation involved. Relocation is disruptive to your life and, if you are married, certainly to the lives of your spouse and children. You also need to consider whether the relocation is to a higher cost-of-living area. In my mind, a gainfully employed executive who is early in his or her career should expect a minimum 12 to 15% bump in compensation to induce a

> If your skills are in high demand and relocation is required, a 20 to 25% bump is not out of line.

move. If less than this, it often is not worth the trouble and risk. If your skills are in high demand and relocation is required, a 20 to 25% bump is not out of line. If you are a recognized star, this percentage can be higher still, maybe in the 30-50% range. At senior executive levels, the most sought after talent may receive compensation packages considerably greater and more performance-based. At some time in your career, you may have the option of trading secure annual cash compensation for a higher performance-based reward. If your primary compensation concerns are not cash-flow related, you may want to accept a greater level of uncertainty for a potential wealth-building performance package that is heavy in stock options.

If you believe an employer's initial offer is fair, you should accept the offer and ask for the agreement in writing. Do not go back and attempt to squeeze out a few more dollars. This can make a poor impression and is not the ideal way to start a new employer relationship. However, if you do not believe the employer's initial offer is fair—based on what you know your skills are worth in the market for this particular role—politely express your concerns one-on-one through the internal corporate recruiter or executive search consultant, ideally providing facts to bolster your request for a compensation increase. In doing so you will want to:

- Be prepared to offer some examples of what similar roles are paying.
- Maintain an accommodating and respectful tone.
- Focus on the one or two elements of the compensation package that are most important to you, not every element.
- Be willing to possibly trade some base salary for performance-oriented incentive upside if the employer is willing to do so.
- Suggest that the employer consider a sign-on bonus or some extra equity to partially cover bonus money or stock options you may be leaving on the table.

If you still do not believe the compensation offer is fair after the negotiations are finished, politely explain to the recruiter or search consultant that you cannot accept the offer, and sincerely thank the person for his or her interest. Express how much you enjoyed meeting and thank him or her for considering you for such an important role. Recognize that there will be disappointment for both the potential employer and those others involved with the process in the client company. The employer and search consultant have invested considerable time and effort in your candidacy, and you have not accepted the offer. Send gracious notes to those involved to help mitigate the disappointment.

As you advance further in your career, compensation discussions can become increasingly complex. Senior level compensation packages often include sizeable base salaries, significant short-term and long-term incentive packages consisting of cash and various forms of stock (equity), defined benefit plans, supplemental executive retirement plans, and a broader array of insurance coverage (medical, dental, vision, life, long-term disability, travel insurance for spouse), and even commuting or housing allowances in some cases.

In these instances, the internal recruiter or executive search consultant will require greater detail about your current or previous employer's compensation and benefits programs. You will want to prepare this information in advance, as it can take some time and effort to gather. You do not want to be taking time to gather and organize this information in the midst of negotiations and risk losing momentum. Often times, the most senior executives will have a compensation consultant assist in the negotiation, either visibly or behind the scenes. The objective of a compensation consultant is to effectively negotiate on your behalf, if required. It is important that the consultant negotiate on your behalf in a manner that helps bring closure based on the formation of a package that both the hiring organization and you view as fair and reasonable. Importantly, do not let your compensation consultant become adversarial or a barrier to closing the deal.

The prevailing attitude regarding the costs of relocation is to cover expenses in such a manner that a senior executive does not end up "out of pocket," or losing money due to a move. While some companies will still purchase a senior executive's current home through the use of a third-party relocation firm, fewer companies now do this due to the turbulence in residential real estate markets over the past decade.

Selectivity

Selecting the right job opportunity is among the most critical career decisions you will make. It has a big impact on your track record, your spouse and your family. Poor decisions often lead to short-term moves, slower advancement, curtailed learning and lower job satisfaction. It also makes for a choppy resume. Although you never know the "right" decision with 100% certainty, there is an approach to making the best decisions.

Imagine yourself in a position of receiving several job offers simultaneously. Lucky you! Compensation is similar for each. Both opportunities are in attractive geographic areas with high quality of life, a reasonable commute, and not too far from extended family. What are the other factors you should consider when assessing which opportunity is the best for you? Below, I highlight a half dozen key factors you will want to consider when assessing a job offer.

Opportunity—Not surprisingly, the actual opportunity you are considering is of primary importance. This, however, is not a simple assessment of title, compensation and major responsibilities. Do you understand the accountabilities and priorities of the role? Are you comfortable with the person you will report to? What is the quality of your staff (if it is a managerial role or leadership role) and the nature of available resources? Against what objectives will your performance be measured? What timeframes are provided to meet those objectives? Is the company open to the idea that you might want to do some things differently? Are you comfortable that your prior experiences and skill sets will enable you to succeed? Are the company's expectations realistic? Do you know why the role is vacant? How long has the organization been trying to fill the role? Is this an opportunity that fits your career game plan and makes your profile more attractive? Do you believe that there are advancement opportunities that will be afforded you? How fully will your skills and experience be utilized in this role? Is there a significant void that you will be filling or will you be one of a number of others in similar roles?

Quality of Organization—Generally, the quality of the organization you are joining should be an important component of your decision. You need to go in with your eyes wide open. Do you really believe in this organization and its products and/or services? Does the organization have an opportunity for growth or improved performance? Do you respect the people who work there? Would you be proud to say you work for this entity? Is it a respected employer? Is it admired by its competitors and customers? Importantly, what does its financial health and stability look like?

There are certain circumstances where you might consider an organization that is less recognized or not quite performing to market expectations. These circumstances might arise because the organization has unrecognized potential and you clearly see an opportunity to make a positive impact or obtain some new skills in areas where your executive profile is weak. Maybe the role is a turnaround scenario or a chance to help grow an emerging, relatively unrecognized but promisingly positioned company. You need to accept such roles recognizing the inherent risks. Hopefully, such risk is being offset by a higher level of performance-based compensation.

People—Do you like your future co-workers, boss, peers and others in the organization who will play a significant role in your happiness and success in the role? What have you observed during the interview process? How were you welcomed and treated? What level of happiness and satisfaction did you encounter during your interactions with employees and executives at the company? What were their values? Were their values in alignment with yours? Were you comfortable in their presence? Do you feel that they were open and candid in answering your questions? Are there people at this organization from whom you can learn? Granted, it is not easy to judge these things during the pressures and time constraints of the interview process, but that may be all you have to go on. Trust your intuition. If there are others in the company you would like to meet or question, there is no harm in asking.

Additionally, take time to check online with Glassdoor.com for further insight. Identify others who have worked at the company recently. Use LinkedIn to locate them and gather their perspectives. Discussion with such folks can be the most candid and insightful conversations of all. Generally, companies that have high employee turnover take years to change. Conversely, if the organization you are considering has received either local or national recognition as a "Best Company to Work For," that is an encouraging sign.

Environment—Work environment is determined primarily by the size, purpose, and setting of an organization. Other environmental factors would include the physical nature of the workspace, staffing, and length of commute. Environment does influence—but should not be equated to—the culture of an organization. The environment is what you go to each day. Culture is about how you work and interact with others and the manner in which business is conducted.

For example, the environment of a large corporation versus that of a small start-up is worlds apart. Working from home is very different than going into an office each day. Similarly, profit versus non-profit, public versus private, domestic versus international are all different environments. It is important to have a good idea of the types of environments where you are comfortable and those where you are less so. When assessing how you might fit into a particular environment, ask yourself questions like:

- Do I prefer an environment where I work closely with others as part of a team or am I more comfortable in an independent role where I can pursue projects without having to be mindful of coordinating with others?

- Do I prefer a more traditional environment with a proven reputation, substantial resources and hierarchical structure or one that is less structured, less predictable and more fluid?

- Do I prefer a service environment where I am measured by the quality of my thinking, creativity, consultative skills, and value-added service delivery (i.e., advertising, public relations, and law) or a business that is focused on a physical product?

Culture—Culture is not the same as environment. This is not to say that culture isn't impacted by environment. It is. However, culture is not about an organization's size, location or setting. Rather, culture is about how an organization conducts its business day-to-day—its beliefs, values and behaviors. In working with different client companies over the years, I have seen how important and different cultures can be. It is typically a major factor in how successful and happy an executive is in his or her job. It's not uncommon for a professional to identify the right job, in the right environment, but not be a cultural fit with an organization.

An organization's culture determines how employees and management interact, solve problems, make decisions, and treat each other and its customers. Often, corporate culture is implied, not expressly defined. It develops over time from the cumulative traits of the people working there. Organizations place varying levels of importance on such things as achieving results, caring for and supporting their employees, diversity, conducting their business in an orderly manner, being open minded and receptive to input or creativity, nurturing an atmosphere where people enjoy their jobs, offering independence and committing to a larger or deeper purpose. All of these factors and more will define the culture of an organization. Increasingly, organizations are making concerted efforts to understand their cultures and shape them. Companies with distinct and attractive cultures are sought after by top professionals. Think about the types of cultures you have worked in previously and where you have flourished. It will be very important throughout your career to join organizations having cultures that are compatible with your personality and work style.

Stability—We have already alluded to the benefits of a stable versus unstable track record (i.e., rapid, multiple moves to different companies) and the impact this can have on the attractiveness of your profile. You have a bit more latitude to make several moves early in your career. However, you do not want to make that an ongoing trend and risk being viewed as a job hopper. If that occurs, potential employers will be hesitant to invest in you and recruiters will be reluctant to present you to their clients.

During the course of a 40+ year professional career, you can expect to change employers on average five times to as many as eight to ten times or more. Ideally, you will move less and build a stellar reputation at a smaller number of quality organizations. This is why it is so important to make proper decisions and moves with an understanding of what the right role, company, environment and culture are for you.

Employers and recruiters do understand that there are circumstances that will be outside of your control which can cause an unexpected move. For example, your company gets acquired, there is a reorganization, changes are made to the management team, or financial pressures force downsizing. However, if these situations occur too frequently, employers and recruiters will question your judgment.

Before accepting a new role and moving to a new employer, be sure to consider the stability of the new company. How long has the management team been in place? How long has your potential boss been with the organization? What is your potential boss's own track record of stability? What is the financial health of the business? Is it investing in the part of the company you would be joining or simply maintaining the business? Has the employer been in the news as a potential acquisition target? How long was your predecessor in the role? What happened to that individual? Is this a new role? If so, has it been properly defined and structured with adequate resources, staffing and expectations in order for you to succeed? Do others in the organization want this position established? Will there be growth opportunities that will keep you satisfied for a longer period of time? Are the industry dynamics and trends supportive?

> Before accepting a new role and moving to a new employer, be sure to consider the stability of the new company.

Transition Management

A significant portion of the search assignments I conducted at Spencer Stuart involved identifying executives able to make sector transitions. While I hesitate to assign an exact percentage to this type of occurrence, 35% feels right. Industry transitions are more easily accomplished with some job functions than others. Functions that tend to be more readily transferrable include marketing, IT, legal, human resources, and finance. Functions that are more industry specific, such as sales or research and development, tend to migrate less successfully. Movement into general management roles across industries occurs most readily where there is a significant common thread between the executive's new role and his or her prior experience. For example, general managers who have worked in the hospitality industry will have a higher probability of success in transitioning to destination resort companies or multi-unit entertainment businesses than they would in moving into classic multi-unit retailing. The more compatible the transition, the greater the likelihood of success. Generally, movements from B2B to B2C companies (and vice versa) are less successful due to the many distinctions between the business models. Sales management, R&D and manufacturing roles transition sectors less often and less successfully because they rely on familiarity with specific customer sets or product and industry and knowledge.

> The more compatible the transition, the greater the likelihood of success.

The potential for an executive to successfully make an industry transition is dependent on his or her ability to learn, adapt and influence others in new settings. Having studied this "Best Athlete" phenomenon, it is evident that those who succeed bring a high level of intelligence, tenacity, ability to deal with ambiguity, willingness to listen, patience, persuasion and influence-building skills, cultural and political sensitivities, change-management aptitude, and innate curiosity.

I have observed that the ability to learn, adapt, and influence is more pronounced in professionals who have had varied job experiences. This trait is often witnessed in executives who have worked across multiple product lines or several companies. This ability to learn, adapt and influence is also seen in executives who have worked with a variety of distribution channels, had international assignments, played different cross-functional roles, held a combination of line and staff positions and have experience in both large and small companies. This is one reason why building a successful executive profile across multiple industries can be seen as a strength. There are, however, risks involved, so such transitions should be thoughtfully executed.

›› Considering an Industry Transition

When considering an industry transition, assess to what degree the opportunity aligns with your core skill sets and competencies as well as your cultural and environmental preferences. Don't be afraid to ask the organization for examples of where and how often it has successfully brought in talent from outside its industry.

The challenges that can be expected with an industry transition include learning about a company's business, industry and customers; becoming familiar with competing organizations; building positive internal working relationships; addressing a lack of talent; adapting to the culture; building credibility; and managing change.

There may also be some unexpected challenges such as entrenched cultures, resistance from support staff, processes and systems with which you are unfamiliar, and hidden corporate sacred cows. You should be sure that the organization you are joining illustrates and communicates support for your new role and provides cultural coaching during your initial months. Ideally, you should have a trusted internal contact with whom to discuss observations, ideas, and roadblocks and to also receive needed feedback from.

›› Learning How to Transition

During the course of your career, you will start new jobs both within your current company through promotions or transfers as well as outside your current company when you move to a new company or industry. You will also likely encounter transitions that are thrust upon you—for example, when your boss moves on and you have a new superior or your current company is acquired. In many respects, these situations are similar to moving into a new role, as there may be a whole new set of expectations that you have to learn about and meet, and new relationships to be built. Over the course of your career, you may experience such transitions on 10 to 20+ or more occasions. This is why learning to transition well is a key skill and should be developed early in your career.

Your success in any job transition relies on your ability to observe, learn, adapt, and influence. Observation requires putting aside your preconceptions, active listening, and asking insightful and timely questions. Beyond observation is learning, which involves understanding the roles of others and how much influence they carry. If you have moved on to a new business, you will need to develop a sound understanding of the products or services, key performance levers, the customer sets and the competitive landscape.

Adapting involves determining what is relevant or irrelevant about your prior experiences and identifying and filling in your knowledge gaps. You will also want to absorb the new culture and adjust your behaviors where necessary. Take time to understand others' motives and points of view. Your ability to adapt will significantly impact your acceptance and rate of growth in a new organization, industry or situation.

To build influence during a transition, you will want to devote time to nurturing important relationships. Waiting weeks or months to do this is a mistake. When meeting with key individuals who will contribute to your success, take the time to understand their objectives, challenges and concerns. Identify who your most likely allies will be as well as those who may be potential obstacles. Separately, identify and utilize all the resources that will allow you to be successful. Pursue some early wins and craft a vision and plan that others can embrace.

When the transition is a job change, the first 100 days in your new role offers a unique window of opportunity to observe, listen, learn, adapt, build relationships, gain alignment and support, and begin to form the team you will need in order to accomplish your goals. Doing so six months or a year later will lead others to wonder where you have been and what you have been doing. You have one honeymoon period when you start a new job, so start "active listening" as soon as possible. Here are some questions to prompt conversations that will help you learn during your transition:

- What all are you and your people responsible for?
- What do you most hope I do?
- What are you most concerned I might do?
- What are your priorities?
- What are the top several things we need to change?
- What is it that is working well? And, not so well?
- What do you believe our biggest opportunities are?

Importantly, take good notes and relate back your findings to those with whom you work closely. Take pains to communicate, communicate, and communicate.

There is a terrific book on this subject written by two highly respected colleagues from Spencer Stuart, Jim Citrin and Tom Neff. It is entitled *You're In Charge, Now What? – The 8 Point Plan*. Jim and Tom are two of the leading CEO recruiters in the industry and experts on leadership. I highly recommend you pick up a copy.

For those of you who are early in your career, success in your initial roles is especially important. You want to build career momentum early on. Do not be overly focused on immediate compensation at this point in your career. Instead, focus on building a strong initial set of core skills, learn how to navigate your way through an organization, and create an early track record of contributions and accomplishments.

How can you build momentum in your initial roles or during transitions? Here are some suggestions:

- Make your boss look like a "star" by making his or her job easier.
- Help others succeed.
- Work hard and carry a great attitude.
- Put in the hours to learn the business. Start strong.
- Build great internal working relationships. Get to know others outside the work environment—company sports

teams, drinks after work, lunch, coffee, co-host a party—all are good ways to get to know people better.

- Look for opportunities to share and present the outstanding work that you do.

- Volunteer for the assignments that nobody else is willing to take.

- Get involved with some committees or task forces to gain visibility, exhibit a capacity to do more, and develop breadth.

)) Handling Departures

Most of us will depart organizations on multiple occasions during the course of our career. It may be the result of being recruited to a new role, or leaving an organization due to a poor job fit, lack of performance, or for circumstances totally outside of our control such as a broad reorganization. The following comments and suggestions are primarily focused on those situations where it is not your decision to depart. In other words, you have been let go.

Unless there is a sudden reorganization, a forced departure should not come as a surprise. If you have been asked to leave due to lack of performance or poor fit, assess why you were let go as best you can. It would be a shame not to learn anything from the situation. Speak with those you have worked with to understand and gain alignment on what they will say about you if asked by potential future employers. Understand how the company will explain your departure.

Ask your company whether it will provide you with the services of an outplacement agency. Outplacement firms and executive coaches help professionals get back on their feet, identify more suitable opportunities and craft a convincing resume. They can also offer assistance with effective interviewing strategies. The key to your next move will be having an understanding of what the next "better" situation looks like and what you will do differently. Otherwise, you risk repeating the same mistakes.

How you behave when leaving an organization can have significant repercussions. You may feel resentment, but don't let it show. How you depart provides the last impression that most people at the company will have of you and will reflect either positively or negatively on your character and reputation. Leave graciously with relationships intact. Do not burn bridges. Remember, your career is likely forty years or more. The odds are pretty good that you will run into some of these same colleagues in the future. Finish with a professional attitude. Nobody likes a sore loser.

If the decision to leave is yours, it is common courtesy to speak first with your immediate superior. Do not have your boss learn of your departure indirectly before you've had a chance to sit down face-to-face. Explain your reasoning in a manner that does not deflate him or

> How you depart provides the last impression that most people at the company will have of you . . .

her. For example, "I've recently been presented with an attractive opportunity outside of our organization that is a very good career move. After giving the opportunity careful thought, I have decided to accept this new role." Then, let your boss know how much you have appreciated his or her support, being a part of the team, and the growth opportunity that he or she has provided.

Should your boss or the organization make a counter-offer, you should stand firm and not encourage it. I have seen on multiple occasions where an executive has announced his or her departure and then received an attractive counter offer and chooses to stay. In my experience, this seldom works out well. Your firm which has made the counter-offer knows that you had one foot out the door and that it will probably lose you in the future. It would be logical for them to start looking. for a potential backup. In other words, you have shown your colors.

As we have seen throughout this chapter, there are a set of fundamental activities that, when mastered, become the building blocks for a successful and effectively managed career: targeted job-search skills, effective networking, continuous resume building, successful interviewing, reference cultivation, negotiation skills, selectivity, and transition management. Many of these skills will be required repeatedly throughout your career. Mastering them will result in optimal outcomes—advancement in position and responsibilities, greater job satisfaction, and enhanced long-term earnings.

Key Chapter Takeaways

» Being aware of and mastering the building blocks of effective career management will allow you to make the most of your intelligence and knowledge, skill sets and experience.

» Being aware of and using these building blocks will help you avoid taking unfortunate career missteps that many executives make.

» You have a given amount of time and energy to pursue a career. These building blocks will ensure that you receive an enhanced ROI (i.e., job satisfaction and long-term earnings) on the time and energy you expend.

Notes:

6

Career Wisdom from Successful Executives

"Careers are a jungle gym, not a ladder."
— *Sheryl Sandberg*

There are few better teachers than those with real-world experience. In this chapter, I have collected the wisdom of successful executives I knew or worked with during my years at Spencer Stuart. They'll share some of their "lessons learned" and "best career advice" from their own professional journeys. I think you'll find it quite illuminating. As I have done throughout the book, these executives' names have been changed so that they can be completely candid.

Linda – Private Equity Portfolio Company CEO

Linda was raised in a blue-collar environment in Michigan. Both her parents were teachers and the importance of education was instilled in her at an early age. After graduating with a business degree from the University of Michigan, she joined a large accounting firm for several years as an auditor and financial consultant. She then returned to school for her MBA at the University of Chicago. Linda then joined a top-tier general-management consulting firm for four years before her travel schedule began to interfere with raising her young family. Instead of exiting the work force, she accepted a marketing and strategy role with one of her clients—a large printing company. This provided her with a more flexible work schedule.

Over the next eight years, she took on further marketing and several general-management roles within the printing company. Linda was then recruited to a competing company where she became the Division President of a $240 million subsidiary. The position involved managing more than 1,200 employees, including staff at three manufacturing facilities (one unionized) and one distribution center, a national sales force, a marketing group and all administrative functions. She went on to be President or Chief Operating Officer of several later companies through 2014, when Spencer Stuart recruited her to be CEO of a an $80 million private equity portfolio company. Here, she built a new senior management team and almost tripled annual revenue before successfully selling the company to another highly regarded private equity firm. She is continuing with this company as its CEO and taking operations to the next level of success.

What I find especially impressive about Linda's background is that—while she admits to naturally being an introvert—she has learned to engage openly in the work environment. She overtly pushed for general management opportunities earlier in her career. She has also been very conscious about making good career decisions and building substance in her profile with each move.

Linda had this to say about the lessons she has learned during her professional journey.

"I have really enjoyed working in a private equity environment. You are able to be much more aggressive than in a more traditional environment when building your team and taking action. We are now growing four times faster than the industry we compete in. Having the right team in place makes all the difference."

"As a young female executive, I had to make choices to be a mother and spend time at home. That is why I left general management consulting. I made the right decision to stay professionally engaged as an executive in a more traditional company setting which provided me more flexibility with my time. This may have limited how fast I progressed at the company, but it worked out well. Professional female friends who made a different decision to leave the work force entirely for a period of time found it difficult to re-engage later on. I'm not sure that many of them ever got their careers back on track. I felt that I personally had to keep a toe in the water."

"As a female executive, I also had my share of unwanted advances by male colleagues. I learned to manage this by having other people present at meetings with these male colleagues, and to not put myself in isolated situations with these male counterparts. The other thing I've learned as a female is that meritocracies are great environments for women. You are judged by your abilities and competence."

"One of the more important lessons I've learned is that despite all of your best efforts on a business or project, it sometimes simply comes down to luck—not anything you did or didn't do. Sometimes you just don't get the right cards to play a strong hand. Some situations are just tough to walk into. It's not about you, your abilities, or your strategy. Running a print business in a digital landscape is not easy. The important thing is to learn from your failures and to not repeat the same mistakes. Don't beat yourself up; move on. I've always been a calculated risk taker. So, I've had some failures. However, that is much better than being happy with the status quo. Some calculated risks work and others may not."

> "Some situations are just tough to walk into. It's not about you, your abilities, or your strategy."

"The best career advice that a boss once provided me was, 'You can do anything, but not everything.' In other words, the magic comes when you pick the handful of things that need to be done, or that have the most impact. The other advice that this boss provided me was, 'You may be the smartest person in the room, but you don't need to let everyone know it. Let others think it is their idea, get them engaged.' When others feel that they are contributing and that their contributions are noticed, this creates inspiration. People want to work for and with other good people who are able to make them feel important and valued."

"One of the best career decisions I made was joining a highly respected general management consulting firm when I was coming out of graduate business school. I was nervous about whether I could cut it in a McKinsey or Boston Consulting Group. I did cut it and gained a lot of confidence in the process. I received great training and learned how to look at a business and understand the key levers, what is important and what is not, and how to communicate to senior executives, boards and managers to convey this information and lay out business cases. Many times you do not need statistical research, but simply to go out and interview customers and employees. The answers for how to get better are often sitting with your employees."

"The other lesson I learned came after one of our consulting clients hired me into a more staff-oriented strategy role. I made the decision to consistently push for an operating and general management role. Had I not pushed, I would have continued to be in a staff role."

"Maybe the best career decision I've made was to accept my current role as CEO of a private equity portfolio company. I'm so thankful that Spencer Stuart called me about this opportunity. It is my first CEO role. I've been able to make bolder decisions in a private equity (P.E.) environment, move more quickly with the business and in building a strong team. The recent sale of this company is one of the most successful investments the P.E. firm has ever had. The new P.E. owner is very highly regarded and I'm looking forward to the next several years. It was a great learning experience to be centrally involved with the sale of the company. Financially, the experience has also been rewarding. If I have any regrets, it's that I did not have the opportunity to get into private equity earlier in my career. It's been a very comfortable fit for me."

"The toughest thing for me to learn over the years has been to improve my ability to engage others. I'm essentially an introvert and can be a bit stand-offish. Having general management responsibilities means being dependent on others to get things done. You need to be approachable, otherwise your team will not come to you with issues. You win people over by looking them in the eye and letting them know why they are important. You do not win employees over through pure intellect."

"Having a good spouse—one who is supportive—is something I've increasingly valued over the years. Being able to bounce your thoughts off of an objective, non-judgmental third party is invaluable. As CEO, you need to have someone to talk to who is not an employee or board member."

"Other things I've learned during my career are that it's okay to ask for help. You do not have to know it all or do it all yourself. Another learning that I would have kept in mind sooner in my career is that it is a lot easier to succeed in a growing market with a good sized addressable customer base."

"The most common advice I give my teams is, 'Know your business metrics and monitor them closely.' And finally, 'Make sure that you have great talent on your team year in and year out.'"

The last several years as CEO of a private equity portfolio company have opened up a new world for Linda. She has been a natural fit for this decisive, results-driven, action-oriented environment. She has clearly made a mark with her recent success. This would not have been possible without her early pushing to receive general management responsibilities.

Jacob – Educational Services Company CEO

For the past ten years of his career, Jacob has been CEO and Board Director of a $2 billion global provider of educational services with 18,000 employees and 140 locations in 36 countries. Bright and well educated, he spent his early career in general management consulting before moving to a direct marketing information services and technology company as head of marketing and business development. After several years in this role, he requested a move within the company to Vice President and General Manager of the company's early Internet Services Group. During the ensuing years, he continued to build on this early success in ecommerce general management with a large B2B products company and a smaller venture-backed online training business. The latter role led to him joining his most recent company in the educational services sector, where he grew the company's revenue from $650 million to $2 billion over fourteen years. During this timeframe, he was promoted from EVP Online to Chief Operating Officer to CEO in just four years.

What sets Jacob apart from other executives is his openness to change and ongoing learning as he has matured in his career. He recognized early on what a powerful force the Internet would become, jumped in early, and used that as a platform for taking on larger and more diverse responsibilities.

During our interview, Jacob offered the following as his most important career lessons:

"When I think back on my career, there were several areas of learning that I believe were critical—the cultivation of my learning agility, building my emotional intelligence, and improving my ability to persuade and appropriately advocate a point of view. My improvement in these areas required that I become more mentally open to feedback. I collected and acted on 360 degree feedback and proactively hired an executive coach to become more effective in dealing with my recent Board. I learned that in order to really change my behavior, it was often necessary to alter my belief system. For example, in my early days as a CEO, I believed that I should have all the answers. However, I learned that you are not always required to have *the* answer, and that oftentimes, the question was really the beginning of a needed dialogue. I learned to not give answers too fast, but to listen more to what others in my organization were saying. I also learned to more openly share what I was working on in order to create greater transparency and alignment across the organization. "

"Another piece of advice that I received was from a mentor who encouraged me to focus on playing to my given strengths and not spend too much time trying to shore up my shortcomings. This mentor commented that I should add members to my team who would shore up these shortcomings, allowing me to spend my time on what I do best. I also learned that in today's swiftly changing landscape, leaders should not become distracted from the core fundamentals of their business. I found that I needed to develop the ability to separate the 'noise' from what is really necessary to the health of the business. Today's businesses and teams require leaders who are mindful, centered, open and authentic. Throughout this timeframe, I have learned to lead with more heart and less intellect. I found that to be an effective leader, you need to repeat the essential messaging around values,

> "Today's businesses and teams require leaders who are mindful, centered, open and authentic."

vision and mission frequently and consistently both internally and externally. The cultural values that I personally espouse are: teamwork, energy, accountability, community, and heart. "

"I believe that the initial twelve years of someone's career should be focused on learning the fundamentals and how to navigate diverse organizational structures as well as building effective work relationships at all levels. I like to see executives who have invested in themselves, build new capabilities, and experience different challenges (turnarounds, high growth, acquisitions, integrations, and startups). I feel strongly that people should not begin their careers in start-up environments."

Jacob's recent fourteen-year journey is impressive. He went from EVP Online in the emerging multichannel education-services space to COO, then CEO and Board Director for what became a $2 billion public company with 18,000 employees and 140 locations in 36 countries. Over this timeframe, his compensation increased 600%. Best of all, with this experience under his belt, he is well positioned for future CEO and Board roles with Internet and multichannel-service companies—all this while still in his early 50s. His profile should be of particular interest to private equity firms as well.

Dave – President, Global eCommerce & Web Strategy for a Large B2B Distributor

Dave graduated from the University of Pennsylvania in 2001 with a degree in Economics and International Relations. He began his career trading for Enron. He then moved to a company offering B2B eCommerce solutions for oilfield-service companies. From 2004 to 2011, he led the eCommerce practice at a general management consulting firm. This consulting experience was invaluable and taught him how to come up to speed quickly in different business situations. Consulting showed Dave how to make convincing presentations to senior management, problem solve, evolve strategies, manage expectations, and build strong interpersonal relationships. He also gained a broad perspective across multiple industry sectors and company cultures.

From consulting, Dave moved to a media company where he led a digital transformation, growing digital revenue from $130 million to $750 million (50% of revenue). When the company came under new ownership, Dave determined that it was time to consider other higher-growth opportunities. In late 2014, Spencer Stuart recruited Dave to be President of Global eCommerce & Web Strategy for a $21 billion distributor of electronic and computer components and SaaS-based services to multiple business sectors. The company has over 470 locations in more than 55 countries. Since joining, Dave has grown eCommerce from $150 million to $500 million (with a goal of $1 billion). He is also leading the company's Internet of Things (IOT) initiative.

Dave is a great example of an executive who has been willing to take calculated risks, transition across multiple industries, and not be afraid of failing. He has built an outstanding track record of "figuring things out" and growing businesses. He brings a mature business perspective despite his relatively young age. This has been gained by trial through fire.

While interviewing Dave, he offered a number of insightful comments:

"The world changes around you during the course of your career. You need to be aware of how the world is changing and the megatrends that are occurring. The pace of change and disconti-nuity come quickly. Those who are observant leverage these meg-atrends to move into higher-growth scenarios. The worst mistake you can make is doing the best you can in a falling tide."

"Determine the experiences you need, and then go out and get them—whether inside your current organization or outside. Have a plan for your career. Look for companies that can catalyze your career. Many people stay at companies too long. You do not want to become complacent and comfortable. You should be receiv-ing new challenges and experiences every two years. There are opportu-nities to do this in your current busi-ness or organization, if you are alert to them. If not, then look outside."

"Early in your career, you should be developing expertise to 'go deep.' Later, you will want to accumulate

> "Determine the experiences you need, and then go out and get them . . ."

experience across multiple sectors, large and smaller organiza-tions, public and private. Large company experience often pro-vides fundamental training, a sense of business discipline, and learning how to get things done in a matrixed structure. Smaller organization experience teaches you to be nimble, resourceful, and self-reliant. Smaller company environments often provide greater opportunity for interaction with senior and top management. This smaller company experience elevated my communication style, clarity, and thinking. I benefited from the mentorship of more senior people at that point in my career."

"Don't be afraid to fail. What is the big deal if you fail? Don't grasp to hold on to what you have. In order to climb a mountain, you have to let go of multiple points of contact. The reality is that no one has it all figured out. Everyone goes through periods of insecurity. Sometimes this creates a lack of belief in putting yourself into situations where you might fail. It's normal to be uncertain about that which is scary or risky. During these times, remember the successful experiences that you have under your belt. Your greatest asset in the world is time. If you do not use it well, you cannot get it back."

> "Your greatest asset in the world is time. If you do not use it well, you cannot get it back."

"In starting a career, new role or challenge, I have learned that it is very important to invest yourself early—burn the candle at both ends, let out all the stops, create early wins, and create tail wind. There is nothing more important than winning early on and building the professional, political and social capital from the start."

"The toughest lesson for me to learn was how to have the 'hard' conversations with peers and authorities who are parallel to your superior. The nature of functional matrixes is that they are going to let you down from time to time. When you decide that there is a problem that you need to elevate, there will also be some risk. I've learned to never approach others with generalities. It is incredibly important to lead with multiple truth points that you understand. Provide others with graceful outs. Suggest that they have someone on their team go and research the problem for one week, determine why the problem happened, and what can be done to resolve it. Explain to your peer, 'What I am seeing is not acceptable and will cause broader failure. If this occurs, I may need to escalate the problem.' Express your expectations in a reasonable manner that allows the other person an opportunity to improve the situation. Soft skills are important in these discussions, as are the facts. People are like snowflakes—no two are alike. Look the other person in the eyes, listen, and let go of your agenda long enough to understand the problem from his or her perspective."

At 39 years of age, Dave's most recent move to his current role puts him center stage in a Fortune 500 company with substantially more resources and responsibility to drive business growth than he has previously experienced. My guess is that several years from now, he will grow global eCommerce revenue to several billion dollars and be a central player in the Internet of Things space. I project that he will continue to take on added responsibilities. Dave is adding significant value to his executive profile, which positions him for an array of opportunities.

Sanjay – Chief Data & Science Officer of Large Insurance Company

Sanjay initially came to the U.S. from India at the age of seventeen. He had only a few thousand dollars in his pocket, and high hopes of getting a college education. A small Mennonite college heard about his situation, and offered him financial support. Sanjay worked thirty to forty hours per week while in school. He also became editor of the campus newspaper and graduated with a degree in Economics. He went on to receive his M.S. in Statistics and Economics before joining a well-recognized, multi-billion bank holding company as a statistician. After four valuable years with this company, he departed to obtain his MBA at a top-five institution. Since then, Sanjay's career has progressed with increasingly more responsible analytical, insight, and data-driven roles in the financial services and insurance industries. Most recently, Sanjay became Chief Science Officer at a Fortune 100 multinational insurance company that operates in 90 countries. He reports directly to the CEO. In this role, he has built a sophisticated, business-oriented, data science department of 180 skilled professionals. Their impact on the company's business has been noteworthy. As a result, Sanjay saw his compensation triple in just over four years.

During my discussion with Sanjay, his exceptional humility, gratitude, self-awareness and authenticity were striking. Here are the insights he shared with me:

"I've been exceptionally fortunate in my life and career that others took an interest in me and that they have supported me. I've had the opportunity to be in some tremendous learning environments and to observe how others inspire their organizations. In my recent role, I was initially the only person on the data science team, and had the opportunity to build a function of 180 talented professionals. We changed the culture of the company by reinventing processes and business models on the basis of advanced analytical insights. By getting others to embrace the power of institutional knowledge through data models, we became a learning culture. The Data Science group became the catalyst for evidence-based decision making across sales, underwriting and claims. This cultural change created financial value and was a factor in the promotion of the CEO of Property & Casualty to CEO of the corporation. Our group's success led to exporting 100 of my team members into visible roles of influence across multiple functions. The impact of this talent and capability is now the centerpiece of how the company is reinventing the business in the face of disruption spurred by data and technology. I gained a lot of personal learning along this journey."

"When I took this role, the mandate from the CEO was to bring about change and build data science capabilities as quickly as possible across the organization. This urgency placed a premium on action and less emphasis on establishing goals and expectations with the C-suite. In retrospect, had I pushed for more precise goals, it might have allowed us to better concentrate our resources and make an even larger financial impact on the business."

> "I've had the opportunity to be in some tremendous learning environments and to observe how others inspire their organizations"

"The other learning point for me was that I needed to take the time to communicate more thoughtfully with the organization. What I said and did in bringing about a substantial transformation, and the influence that I had caused a range of emotions. I learned to be more conscious of person-to-person interactions, acknowledging others, and having conversations that struck a balance of being tough but also fair and constructive. Doing this also meant understanding the fears and issues of others."

"Another learning that I took away from this particular team building role was the importance of looking beyond a hire's skill sets to better understand his or her cultural fit. It is a challenge finding great data science talent as these people are in high demand. Finding those with strong interpersonal skills and the right cultural fit is even tougher. If I had it to do over again, I would strike more of a balance between skill sets and cultural fit."

"There are other learnings from earlier in my career that I have passed on to members of my team. Early in my career, I wanted to see the meaning in my work every day. I had to teach myself that not everything you do is going to have perfect meaning. I saw that some of the less meaningful things I was asked to do became 'enablers' for more meaningful activities I would later do. And, to be honest, I left a prior employer prematurely for this reason. Patience is sometimes required. You need to stay with a task or role for a proper amount of time, roll with some of the punches, and have the discipline to see things through. GRIT (Guts, Resilience, Initiative, Tenacity) is really important. Do not give others the power to affect your confidence and enthusiasm, or to determine what is possible for you. Ask what you can do to create the future that you want. Luck plays a role, but is not enduring. Continued growth and continuous learning, course correcting, pushing your boundaries are what is important."

"I had to teach myself that not everything you do is going to have perfect meaning."

"I did not come to the U.S. from India with any understanding of the culture, nor what it means to be a top-notch leader. In many ways, the culture here was more subtle than what I was accustomed to. In my first role here following school, when I would pass someone I recognized in the hallway at work they would ask, 'How are you doing?' It took me a while to figure out that they were simply being friendly and saying 'hello,' not really asking about how my life was going. In India, we freely invite others to our home to get to know them better. In the U.S. this can appear too forward. I learned instead to invite others for coffee versus to my home for dinner. The other cultural learning curve for me was in understanding the gamesmanship that happens in larger companies, the positioning and posturing that are sometimes beneficial. I had to learn how to adapt my communication and style to the context of a given situation, and to do so with authenticity. At times, you have to be agile enough to play hardball. When you play in the NFL, you have to be able to both take and give some hits in the appropriate manner."

"In the U.S. work culture, how you present yourself has tremendous impact on how others think about you as well as themselves, especially if part of your team. Everything you say and do impacts others when you are in a role of leadership. This has an impact on others' sense of self and their morale. Something as simple as not acknowledging one of your staff members in an elevator has unintended repercussions. I learned to show more sincerity and to be more expressive and to present my thoughts more openly. This sharing helped inspire others."

"Another component of leadership and managing that I learned is understanding how assertive to be and when. Push too much in the wrong way and others can become quite uncomfortable. Yet, if you do not push hard enough things may not improve, or opportunities might be missed. Early in my career, I was perceived as polite and thoughtful, and there were times when I could have been more direct. Having the ability to define boundaries but push on the edges is something I learned by better assessing the probability of success versus the cost of being more forceful. I also came to realize that some issues have a time dimension and that you should not push things too far ahead of the organization's adoption curve."

As a next step in his already accomplished career, Sanjay is positioning himself for a significant line-management role in the insurance or financial services industries. His intelligence, authenticity, energy, team building, communication, and transformational skills are assets for this next leap. His deep data science acumen and experience is well suited for today's business environment.

Andrew – New Product and Innovation Entrepreneur

Andrew, a successful entrepreneur, offers yet another distinct career path and set of lessons learned. Andrew was the first generation in his family to receive a college education, graduating with an accounting degree and obtaining his CPA. He later returned to school for his MBA at Harvard where he was the youngest in his class. On leaving Harvard with his MBA, he joined a highly regarded consumer package foods company in brand marketing for five years before building a small marketing consulting business over the ensuing five years. After this, he was recruited by Spencer Stuart into a series of Chief Marketing Officer positions. Sixteen years into his career, Andrew decided that he wanted to leverage the breadth of his marketing experience across multiple sectors and build a second consulting company in Detroit focused on strategic innovation. Over the next twelve years, he built the business to fifteen consultants, acquired a new products research company, and opened offices in Chicago and Toronto before selling his business to a large international market research and consulting firm.

In the ensuing several years, Andrew's focus shifted to conservation and sustainability, economic revitalization, health and quality of life issues. He began helping a variety of organizations, large and small, for-profit and not-for-profit, to grow and make a difference. Before he knew it, what began as solo project work evolved into an expanding team of colleagues and clients with a scope extending outside the Midwest. He found the work to be very fulfilling and has formed a strategy consulting company with a social mission mindset.

What stands out about Andrew's background is that he has not been afraid to follow his passion. Early on in his career, he realized that his strengths were an ability to mesh right- and left-brain thinking, an advanced understanding and inquisitiveness about consumers, and an entrepreneurial spirit. He loves identifying problems and opportunities and building solutions.

When asked about the lessons he had learned throughout his career, Andrew offered the following:

"I did not realize how valuable the connections I formed at the consumer package foods company after business school could later become. It was an extraordinary environment populated with very high caliber individuals who went on to find success. A lesson I wish I'd learned earlier was to further build and maintain those relationships. These relationships can be so helpful in providing future business introductions and recommendations for resources as you grow a small business. These connections are also invaluable for bouncing ideas off of or discussing particular business challenges with others you consider personal advisors."

> "A lesson I wish I'd learned earlier was to further build and maintain those relationships."

"Another lesson I learned with time was to play to your passion, interests and strengths. This requires that you try new things and trust your gut. It can take some time and multiple experiences to recognize these things. You do not always have to be in a hurry. Some very good things take time in bubbling to the surface. You should not be too quick in pulling the trigger on a current role and jumping to a new company. Very often you will discover continued opportunities for learning in your current organization if you look, make your wishes known, and show some initiative."

"Any one person has only so many moves to new companies that he or she can make and still maintain credibility."

"Be willing to fail while searching for your inner passion and discovery of who you are. I learned some important things about myself in the process. Namely, that I love people and understanding people in relation to marketing, innovation, and the creation of opportunities. I'm able to bring a right-brain, left-brain perspective to problem solving. This knowledge is what led to the formation of my prior consulting company and the current firm that I have recently formed."

Now in his mid to late 50s, Andrew has established financial security and has the freedom to pursue his interests in making the world a better place. His focus is conservation and sustainability, economic revitalization, broader quality of life issues. He has begun to use his considerable talents to build yet another services firm to assist a variety of non-profit organizations. Given Andrew's passion and willingness to try new things, it will be very interesting to see where this leads to next.

░ ░ ░ ░

As I interviewed these five executives for this chapter of *The Proactive Executive*, I was particularly struck by how consistently their comments concerning "lessons learned" and "best advice ever received" were aligned with much of the underlying advice found in this book. These five executives are examples of the career benefits gained through the core principles outlined in *The Proactive Executive*. So much can be learned from asking others about the professional and life lessons they have learned and the advice that has shaped their careers. I encourage you to build strong professional relationships and ask these same questions of successful executives *you* respect. I promise they will make for great lunch conversations that, in some cases, may shift the course of your career.

Key Chapter Takeaways

》》 Spend the formative part of your career, the initial 6 to 12 years, learning business fundamentals and building a foundation of key skill sets—both technical and interpersonal.

》》 Believe in yourself, and let others know how you want to advance your career.

》》 Wholeheartedly pursue continuous learning.

》》 Be willing to take calculated risks. Understand that failure is part of growth.

Notes:

7

An Inside Look at the Executive Search Process

"I am convinced that nothing we do is more important than hiring and developing people. At the end of the day you bet on people, not on strategies." — *Lawrence Bossidy*

Executive search has evolved over the decades to playing a very critical role in today's global business environment, especially in identification, attraction, assessment and hiring of talented leadership for companies and organizations ranging in size from tens of millions of dollars in revenue to hundreds of billions of dollars. The executive search industry started in 1946 and gained rapid legitimacy as an offshoot of general management consulting. Spencer Stuart was founded in 1956 as one of the first retainer-based executive search firms. In the late 80s and early 90s, a handful of high profile CEO searches for Fortune 500 companies brought widespread publicity, attention, and increased acceptance. The "War for Talent" in the mid-2000s led to global demand for executive search services and rapid industry growth.

There are literally thousands of executive search firms in the U.S. ranging from small boutiques to large, heavily resourced global networks. The best executive search firms are recognized for providing the objectivity, industry expertise, resources, global reach and access to top talent which today's companies need. They have developed cutting edge systems and processes to quickly identify and attract the best talent for their clients, whether a functional leadership role, CEO, or Board Director need. Because the top retainer firms have access to client roles ranging from $250,000 to millions of dollars in compensation, it is important that you understand how these firms work and that you develop targeted relationships with the right executive search consultants.

It is important to recognize that there are different types of placement organizations:

Types of Search and Placement Firms

Placement Agencies and Staffing Companies—These types of organizations are often industry or job specific. They offer candidates—from administrative assistants to senior professionals—the opportunity to gain access to companies in one of two ways: on a temporary basis or on a temporary-to-hire basis. Assignments can last anywhere from one day to six months or longer. These organizations can also offer full-time temporary assignments.

Executive Search Firms—There are two types of Executive Search Firms: contingency and retainer-based. Both offer permanent placement solutions. There are varying levels of quality and specialization in the Executive Search industry. These firms range from large global firms that are quite specialized and focused on recruiting functional and general management leadership in the C-suite and at the Board levels and smaller boutiques that may have five or fewer employees, operate locally, and have a very specific industry or functional focus.

- **Contingency firms**—This type of firm is the best fit for mid-level managers and directors. The compensation for roles presented by contingency firms is generally in the $90,000 to $250,000 range, depending on the firm. Contingency firms are paid by the client only when a placement occurs. Often, there will be multiple contingency firms competing for a single placement on a given assignment. These firms generally do not have exclusive rights to a particular job search. The quality and thoroughness of contingency firms can vary significantly. If your compensation falls in the dollar range described above, you will want to identify local and regional contingency firms that are relevant to your career. You should be able to identify such firms by doing some online research and speaking with your peers.

■ **Retainer-based firms**—This type of firm generally handles specific, exclusive assignments with compensation packages that range from $250,000 to multiple millions of dollars, depending on the search firm. As I've mentioned, Spencer Stuart was positioned at the high end of this spectrum. Retainer-based firms are paid by the client organization, typically over the initial three months of the assignment. This type of search firm commits to bringing substantial resources, and a high level of industry or functional knowledge and professional support. It delivers a thoroughly vetted slate of top candidates and has extensive databases and relationships with senior leadership talent across industry sectors.

Should you be an executive whose compensation is approaching the $250,000 level or higher, even if you are not looking, you should consider requesting that your resume and relevant information (i.e., compensation details, relocation parameters, and career objectives) be added to their databases. You never know when that one ideal, life-changing opportunity might arise. Initiate and nurture relationships with these top firms. They are able to provide timely and objective market and career insight. You should selectively meet their search consultants or key research associates who align with your interests and experience. This can be a challenge at times, as these consultants are very busy serving clients, which is their first priority. However, the more attractive your profile, the higher the likelihood that you will receive their attention and be privy to a more personal relationship with them.

If one of these consultants should call you, return their call promptly and respect their time, as they will yours. If you are not interested in the position they describe to you, explain why and then try to help them by offering the names of other suitable, high quality prospects. They will remember this and think about you more readily in the future when the next "right" opportunity comes along. Your interaction with a true search professional should be a two-way relationship.

The Executive Search Process

The executive search process consists of five broad steps—the client briefing, identification of potential prospects, attraction and education of preferred prospects, formal assessment and presentation of candidates, and final referencing and closure. A typical executive search process involves the contact and screening of 75 to 120 executives on average. That number can approach 300 contacts or higher on challenging searches. That list will produce a "long list" of 12 to 15 prospects. These 12 to 15 prospects are further vetted, interviewed by the executive search firm, and early referenced to yield an initial slate of 4 to 6 candidates. If the search has been properly executed, typically the initial slate or short list will produce two finalist candidates.

Identification of potential candidates is accomplished through querying the search firm's database, a review of similar assignments in the recent past, ideas collected from colleagues on monthly practice calls, proactive identification of executives in a target list of desirable companies, and thorough networking with industry executives friendly to the search firm. LinkedIn profiles are reviewed for searches primarily at the VP level or lower. To date, search firm databases are more productive at the very senior and top levels of management.

Prior to a candidate's meetings with the client, a good search consultant will provide the executive with background information on who the executive will be meeting, their backgrounds, information about the client company, and any further insights that may prove helpful. If necessary, a good search consultant will provide any required coaching before the client meeting—especially with

SEARCH PROCESS: *Five Broad Steps*

COMMENCE (Weeks 1–2) ▼

ASSESS NEEDS AND DEVELOP TAILORED BLUEPRINT

-Meet client to determine required skills/experience for role
-Analyze challenges unique to organization and the role
-Prepare customized position and candidate specification
[Consultant responsibility]

IDENTIFY (Weeks 3–7) ▼

IDENTIFY TARGET COMPANIES AND POTENTIAL PROSPECTS

-Examine organizations with relevant skill-sets
-Develop long list of organizations to serve as likely sources
-Present long list of prospects
-Speak to third-party sources to identify and qualify prospects
[Consultant/Research Associate]

DEVELOP (Weeks 8–15) ▼

ATTRACT AND EVALUATE CANDIDATES

-Engage prospects to determine interest in the role
-Conduct competency-based interviews against the position
 specification
-Assemble the short list
-Periodic progress reports with client
[Consultant]

PRESENT (Weeks 16–19) ▼

PRESENT CANDIDATES FOR CLIENT INTERVIEWS

-Prepare detailed candidate reports for 4-6 most qualified executives
-Conduct preliminary reference checks
[Consultant/Research Associate]

COMPLETE (Weeks 20–24)

COMPLETE THE SEARCH AND POST-SEARCH FOLLOW-UP

-In-depth referencing and background checks
-Facilitate or lead compensation discussions/negotiation
-Regularly communicate with client placement during transition
-Conduct client satisfaction survey
[Consultant]

respect to interview effectiveness of the candidate. It is not infrequent for search consultants to come across candidates who have not done a lot of interviewing, or who have not interviewed recently.

Candidate reports are sent by the search firm to clients ahead of onsite interviews. The reports address:

- The candidate's fit with regards to experience and skill sets required for success in the role
- A review of the executive's track record, achievements, and transitions
- An assessment of cultural fit with the client company
- The executive's sufficiency level with respect to required critical competencies for success in the role and organization
- Reference input
- Comment on the executive's level of interest in the opportunity as well as why he or she is interested
- Compensation details
- Relevant personal information—openness to relocation, housing needs, special schooling needs

The chart on page 169 is an exhibit outlining the five broad steps involved in a typical retainer-based executive search engagement. You should especially note the activities involved in each step of the process, the approximate duration of each step, and participant roles and responsibilities.

Popular Questions about the Search Process

The three questions I'm most often asked by executives wanting to better understand executive search are: "What should I expect?,""How do I identify the right recruiters to work with?" and "How do I go about establishing relationships with the right search consultants?" The following will provide you some guidance.

What should I expect from a search firm that is presenting me as a potential candidate?

- A thoughtfully crafted and insightful position description
- Honesty, candor, and reasonable responsiveness (1-3 business days)
- A briefing prior to each round of client interviews and a debriefing (phone or email) within several days following the interviews
- The expectation that the consultant or research associate will close the loop with you if you are not the placement and provide helpful feedback for the future

How do I best identify search consultants with whom to work?

- Start by tapping your own network.
- Scan recruiter directories. A great resource for doing this can be found at www.customdatabanks.com. Using this service will cost you only $100 to $150.
- Review recruiting firm websites for the profiles of their search consultants.
- Search LinkedIn for the profiles of recruiters.
- Obtain referrals from trade groups and industry associations. Recruiters are often members of relevant associations.

What should I do to develop relationships with search firms?

- Don't wait until you need a recruiter to develop a relationship.
- Target your overtures to consultants and research associates who do work in your job function or industry.
- Contact research associates. Over the years, these individuals have taken on greater responsibility for search execution. They share responsibility with their search consultants for servicing clients and delivering successful searches. Unlike consultants, they have limited responsibility for client management and candidate assessment, and no responsibility for business development. They tend to work

on a greater number of searches at one time because of this. As such, they can be good initial contact points for executives looking to establish a search firm relationship.

- Do not cold call search firms. This will waste their time and yours.

- Prior to contacting a targeted consultant or research associate, you should send your resume to them with an appropriate cover letter, and suggest that you will call them the next week for a brief 10-minute introduction. I provide a good example of a cover letter on the following page.

- Ensure that you have accurate and up-to-date information in their database.

- When possible, establish a face-to-face presence. Ask to stop by their office for a ten-minute meeting when you are in their city. This should occur after you have developed a phone or Internet connection with them.

- When they call you about an opportunity, be candid as to your fit and interest in the position. If it is not the right role for you, make a genuine effort to try and be helpful—this will be remembered.

- If you become aware of an executive search that is about to be conducted within your firm or the industry, give your favorite recruiter a call and alert him or her of the new assignment opportunity—provided it is not confidential. Bringing in new searches is part of their livelihood. They will appreciate the lead and remember you for it.

- Be easy to work with!

Effective Email Cover Letters to Search Firms

An effective cover letter should be several paragraphs long (a half to three-quarters of a page) and provide the search consultant or research associate necessary information for understanding the types of assignments you would be a good fit for. The cover letter also provides essential information to be added to the firm's database for the benefit of its colleagues. Below is an example of a cover letter that makes it easy for the search consultant or research associate to work with you in an efficient manner.

(First Name),

Sam Jones, who you know, encouraged me to contact you.

I recently finished a rewarding 15-year run at DIGICORP LLC, a $100 million digital media and content company in Austin. Over the years, I led multiple acquisitions and integrations. In recognition of my effectiveness, I was consistently promoted, ultimately becoming COO the last three years. In this role, I was accountable for all domestic and international operations across 25 countries.

In 2014, we successfully sold the company to a private equity firm for $300 million, and I stayed on to assist the transition in ownership. I am now seeking a COO or Operating CFO role with a $50 million to $250 million growth-oriented company. The industries I am interested in are digital content, digital media and technology, B2B2C digital services, and digital information services. Please also be aware that I:

- Am willing and able to relocate.
- Do not have a non-compete.
- Previously earned a total compensation package (base salary, bonus, and LTIP) in the $750,000 range. However, I am willing to trade off cash for equity and am more interested in the quality of the growth opportunity.

My resume is attached. I would appreciate 10 minutes of your time for an introductory phone conversation and will give you a call next week. Additionally, if you would kindly refer this cover letter and resume to any others in your organization (consultants and research associates) who might have interest, it would be appreciated.

Very truly yours,

John Smith

Key Chapter Takeaways

》 Establish and maintain close relations with targeted executive search consultants and research associates. Often, the right research associates will be easier to reach and have a broader appreciation for relevant searches that the search firm is conducting related to your functional or industry experience.

》 Remember that a relationship with a search consultant is a two-way street. Be candid, helpful and respect his or her time. As a result, the consultant will more likely treat you in the same manner.

Notes:

8

"What If?" Scenarios

"There is no education like adversity."

— *Disraeli*

Over the years, I've had many, many discussions with executives about unexpected scenarios that they have faced in their careers—acquisitions, firings, layoffs, grumpy co-workers, etc. What has been most interesting to me is how each of them has responded to these challenges.

The following twelve scenarios are some of the more common challenges that executives face during their careers. Many executives do not give these situations any thought until they find themselves confronted with them. My intent in this chapter is to share some of these challenges and provide suggestions about how to cope with them. Such situations can be very disconcerting. It is important to not react too quickly, or overreact. You must take time to understand what has caused the problem. Often, your response will become evident as you begin to understand the dynamics behind the challenge.

Before we get more specific, here are some general suggestions:

- After developing a sound understanding of the dynamics and cause of the unexpected challenge, determine what this means for your current role and career. Determine whether the challenge is worth reacting to.

- Talk with colleagues and professional acquaintances who have been in similar situations, ask how they responded, and learn from their experiences.

- Formulate a response or plan for dealing with the challenge and share this with a trusted colleague, mentor, coach, or a familiar recruiter for his or her feedback. You do not want to act in a vacuum.

As you read through the following scenarios, ask yourself what you would do.

My boss was just fired

If you find yourself in this position, try and learn the specific reasons why your superior was let go. Have a discussion with your departed superior to see what you're able to learn. Are the reasons specific to his or her performance or personality? Ask yourself, "How directly will this reflect on me?" If you were a strong performer for the organization prior to your departing boss's arrival, you may have nothing to be concerned about. On the other hand, if your superior hired you into the company and his or her business or department has not been performing, you may also be at risk of losing your job. If this is the case, have a direct conversation with your boss's superior and get a read on the company's ongoing commitment to you. Certainly, your own personal performance up to this time is a factor. If you are receiving uncertain signals about your good standing following your boss's departure, you should immediately begin to mount a discrete and confidential job search.

> Have a discussion with your departed superior to see what you're able to learn.

On the other hand, if your boss has been recruited to another opportunity, you will want to understand the nature of the opportunity he or she has been recruited to. If your boss thinks highly of you, he or she may want to bring you along with them. However, before saying "yes," determine whether doing so is a sound and stable career move. Do not blindly follow a prior boss because you like and respect him or her. Sometimes a superior may be leaving your current organization one step ahead of the axe coming down. If this is the case, you need to determine to what degree the departure is a reflection of concerns about your boss, versus the business. There is a distinction between the business outgrowing your boss as opposed to a business that is not performing.

My sponsor left the company

A sponsor is typically a more senior executive who either formally or informally watches out for your best interest in the organization and talks positively about the work that you are doing with others. He or she can volunteer you to others for positions that open up within the company, or alert others of your interest in new roles and vouches for your good standing. A sponsor is *not* a day-to-day mentor who works with you, trains you, or helps you navigate the work day complexities of the organization.

Should your sponsor leave the company, you will want to ask him or her whether there is someone else in the company who thinks well of you and might be willing to informally act as your sponsor. Consider your prior sponsor's suggestion of an alternative sponsor, and determine whether you are comfortable with the idea. If so, don't immediately ask outright unless this other person is already familiar with you and favorably inclined towards you. You might suggest, at the right time, that your mentor approach the potential sponsor on your behalf. As best you can, make the potential sponsor aware of key projects you are working on and reinforce your value and skill sets. Take actions to make this executive more successful, or his or her job easier. Determine how you are able to support

> Take actions to make this executive more successful, or his or her job easier.

this person and his or her mission or plan. Establish a professional bond before you request support or guidance from this person. The ideal scenario is to have several sponsors throughout your organization, so that if one leaves you still have someone looking out for your best interest.

I was passed over for a promotion

Few things are more disheartening in your career than being passed over for a promotion. There are three ways you can respond to this type of event:

- Stick your tail between your legs and quietly get over it
- Become openly emotional, upset or angry
- Express your disappointment, but support the person who did get the job. Ask your superior what you can do to position yourself more favorably for the next promotion opportunity.

Here's a poignant story as told by *Newsweek* about someone many people consider the best basketball player of all time. In 1978, Michael Jordan was just another kid in the gym, along with 50 or so of his classmates, trying out for the Emsley A. Laney High School varsity basketball team. There were 15 roster spots. Jordan—then a 15-year-old sophomore who was only 5'10" and could not yet dunk a basketball—did not get one. His close friend, 6'7" sophomore Leroy Smith, did. The team was in need of his height. "It was embarrassing not making the team," Jordan later said. He went home, locked himself in his room and cried.

Then he picked himself up and turned the cut into motivation. "Whenever I was working out and got tired and figured I ought to stop, I'd close my eyes and see that list in the locker room without my name on it," Jordan would explain. "That usually got me going again."

If you have been passed over for a position by your company, reflection and resilience are your best response. If you have a good reputation at the company and are performing your job well, double-down your efforts, improve where you are considered to have shortcomings, and look for visible opportunities to show

how much you are growing. If, on the other hand, you learn that the likelihood of being promoted in the future continues to diminish, you should self-reflect and ask yourself whether the role and company are misaligned with who you are and the skill sets you have to offer.

I'm having a difficult time with a coworker

The answer to this scenario is specific to the situation. It may be that your coworker has issues with many people. If this is the case, don't take it personally. Make an effort to build a more positive relationship by understanding what the other person's objectives and concerns are, and what motivates him or her. Try to make your coworker part of the solution. If this is not working, take note of specific examples of where his or her lack of support and cooperation are not aligning with the company's objectives. Sit down with the individual and talk about these examples. Give him or her an opportunity to respond. If this still does not work, let the coworker know that if things do not improve, you will need to raise his or her lack of support to another level. Only you can decide how comfortable you are in doing so.

Work environments are naturally competitive. Everyone wants to shine, be noticed and promoted. However, in instances when competitive behavior by coworkers is taken to an extreme and impacts your performance and reputation—or the good of the overall organization—you need to respond more immediately and directly with specific examples of the person's poor or unsupportive behavior. Suggest healthier behaviors and actions that will help diffuse the situation.

> Make an effort to build a more positive relationship by understanding what the other person's objectives and concerns are . . .

The company has stopped investing in my business

Many executives who have been in an operating role have had their budgets cut due to financial pressures that their company may be facing—perhaps a need for funding in another part of the organization or weakening demand for the company's products or services due to a market downturn or shift. Many times, these might be temporary conditions that will cycle through.

The real issue arises if your business has been designated as not worthy of continued funding and investment at a level which you believe is necessary. If this situation arises, you are better off recognizing the problem sooner rather than later. If you find yourself with considerably fewer resources or a declining market, it will become significantly more challenging to make an impact on the business. If spending has migrated to another part of the organization, you should explore whether there is an appropriate role in that area and try to reposition yourself into another healthier situation. You might also entertain cross-functional roles that move you into new areas where you can further build your profile and broaden your experience and skill sets. This could even be a lateral developmental career move. If none of these options are available to you—and you want to further build your career—begin to put out feelers for more suitable roles in your organization, at other companies and perhaps in other industries.

My company was acquired by a foreign-owned firm

Working for a foreign owned firm, either by choice or because your company has been acquired by a non-domestic entity, brings a unique set of challenges. Chances are that the power structure will reside outside the U.S. and have significant influence over the business. Your boss may even be in another country. If this happens to you, try and understand the history of other U.S. acquisitions the foreign parent company has made. They may have a history of being hands-off with the acquired entity, or very hands-on and install their own leadership. Talk with others in your firm and, as best you can, project what the future looks like. Remain long enough to begin reading the tea leaves. Don't jump prematurely. If the future begins to look questionable, you can discretely start looking for other opportunities.

> Don't jump prematurely. If the future begins to look questionable, you can discretely start looking for other opportunities.

Conversely, if the foreign-owned parent company is hands off, investing capital into your business, or provides expansion opportunities, you will likely want to stay and let the situation play out. In these instances, you need to forge strong bonds with colleagues abroad and ideally a sponsor within the foreign headquarters. You will want to be visible in person at headquarters as often as is warranted and productive.

While this scenario can be a nice growth experience for an executive, such a role is not for everyone. In order to thrive in this scenario, an executive needs to be comfortable handling cultural differences and be politically attuned, study the new culture, and perform consistently at a high standard. Executives who have previously lived and worked internationally are more apt to be successful in these types of situations. If you have not had such experience, evaluate the risk/reward balance of your situation. If you have not read a book entitled *When Cultures Collide – Leading Across Cultures,* by Richard D. Lewis, I recommend that you order a copy. He provides an insightful and practical review of business cultures, practices, values and behavior patterns in 60 countries around the globe.

My company was just acquired by a private equity firm

If your company has recently been acquired by a private equity firm, there is a good chance that it will soon leave its imprint on the business. This is especially true if your employer has been a public entity. If your CEO has been effective in selling the company for top dollar, there is a good chance that he or she may soon be cashing out and a new CEO will soon be arriving. Oftentimes, the new CEO will want to bring in some new managers that he or she knows and trusts. You need to keep in mind that the new private equity owner is highly motivated to create further value rapidly and sell—or take the company public—ideally within a three to five-year timeframe.

Private equity companies generally are not a patient breed nor reluctant to make key personnel changes if their objectives—sometimes unreasonable—are not being met. These organizations are about creating value for their investors and themselves. They care significantly less about nurturing people's careers. If you are offered a role with the acquired firm, along with some potential equity, you may well want to consider staying. Those executives who do well in private equity scenarios are not only very skilled in their roles, but tend to have thick skins, be action-oriented, impatient for results, willing to put in long hours (i.e., sacrifice work-life balance), and make quick decisions on staff effectiveness.

> Those executives who do well in private equity scenarios are not only very skilled in their roles, but tend to have thick skins . . .

Over the years, I learned that there are "good" private equity firms that operate with values and transparency and "bad" firms that are less focused on building sustainable companies and more focused on flipping a company for a quick buck.

Some firms are considerably more supportive of their management teams than others (although every private equity firm website talks about how closely, supportively, and collaboratively they work with their management teams). Before deciding to participate with a private-equity owned portfolio company, you should carefully investigate the reputation of the private equity firm, its track record, operating style, and integrity.

Although not a "What if...?" scenario, some professionals *choose* to work for private equity firms for the potential wealth generation that results from successful liquidity events. In my mind, the move to a private equity portfolio company tends to make the most sense for senior executives who are more advanced in their careers and who have built an attractive and marketable set of skills and experience. These individuals join private equity firms in one of two primary capacities—either as an operating partner in the private equity firm or as an executive in a portfolio company.

Operating partners within a private equity firm will oversee a single or multiple portfolio companies and often sit on the boards of these companies. They will also have responsibility for conducting due diligence on potential acquisitions, if their experience is relevant. The operating partner

> Some professionals choose to work for private equity firms for the potential wealth generation that results from successful liquidity events.

role may well extend into future acquired portfolio companies and involve an ongoing relationship with the private equity firm as long as the operating partner is successful and creates value. If a senior executive becomes involved with private equity by joining a portfolio company as CEO or as a key functional leader, often his or her involvement will tend to be shorter term (as compared to the longer-term relationship of the operating partner). As a top executive in a portfolio company, your position may last only until there is a liquidity event, at which time you will want to cash out your equity. Additionally, quite frequently the new private equity firm will put in its own management team. However, it is also possible that the new private equity firm will want to keep you on the team and offer you further equity to stay.

For younger professionals just out of business school, private equity is a whole different matter. While the money and wealth-building opportunities are attractive, my personal feeling is that it is an uncertain way to start building a career. My observation is that private equity firms are not dissimilar to law firms that hire the best and brightest students as associates, work them tooth and nail, and keep only the very top performers. If an associate does not make the cut, he or she can move on to another private equity firm. While associates may develop their analytical skills in the private equity world, the downside of this early career choice is there is little opportunity to build further core skill sets that are relevant to running a business. If your career in private equity does not advance, you are ill-positioned to compete in the broader job market. I would much prefer to see young professionals build a marketable set of business skills and enter the private equity realm later in their careers when they bring more value and have more fully formed skill sets, greater business perspective, and a broader network of contacts. Those executives who are fortunate enough to become partners in private equity firms are there because of their operating track record, ability to source deals, personal access to funding, or their contacts and network.

My career has stalled

This is not at all an uncommon scenario. Even the best, brightest and most accomplished executives will have plateaus at various points during their career or timeframes during which their career may move more slowly. The key is to assess whether the plateau seems to be permanent or temporary in nature. If you believe it is temporary, be patient. One of the worst mistakes you can make is jumping ship prematurely. Let others know of your desire to make greater contributions to your organization, and ask how you can position yourself for emerging opportunities. Importantly, build sponsors and advocates ahead of time.

If you believe that the plateau is more permanent—and you are not willing to live with it—I suggest that you have a direct conversation with your superior to learn why this is the case. If it cannot be resolved to your satisfaction, it may well be time to begin looking for greener pastures. The other option you might consider—if your company is willing—is to make a lateral move into another function. While this may not be an upward move, it can provide an opportunity to learn new skill sets and form a more well-rounded view of the company and business. This may open up opportunities in the future for which you are uniquely qualified. Minimally, you have added some differentiating aspects to your executive profile.

If a lateral opportunity is not available, you should begin to think about either moving to a more suitable environment in a new company or industry. The benefits of potential industry transitions are more fully discussed in Step 3, pages 42-43; and Step 5, pages 137-140.

I've had several quick job moves, mostly for reasons outside of my control

If you find yourself in this situation, there are two things you will want to consider. First, how can you effectively convey your transition story without appearing to denigrate the companies you have worked with previously? Second, what can you do to ensure that your next move is of longer tenure?

In conveying your transition story, be honest and straightforward. If there is earlier experience on your resume that exhibits longer tenure, you will want to draw attention to this. Acknowledge that recent moves have been quicker than you would have liked and mention briefly the circumstance. Some of this movement you may be able to position as being the result of the disruption seen across so many industry sectors in recent years. However, don't dwell on the negative. Instead, discuss what you learned from these experiences in a positive light. Rehearse your transition story with trusted colleagues.

The other important topic that you will want to think about is, "How can I make better job decisions in the future?" You need to give careful thought as to what your next move should look like. You will want to find a more secure setting where you can build your executive profile within a single organization for four to seven years. You will need to be even more deliberate in the decision-making process. Making the right job decisions throughout your career is one of the most important skills you can develop. This topic is discussed in detail in Step 4, Section 8, "Master the Ten Building Blocks of Successful Career Management."

I now find myself managing people old enough to be my father or mother

In today's digital and technology-driven world, this is a fairly common occurrence, especially for millennials. Such situations can initially be a bit awkward, especially if the older members of the team or department have been with the organization for many years. If you find yourself in this scenario, you will want to sit with each of your key people and outline what your group has been asked to accomplish and why each individual's particular role is important to achieving success. Ask for the input of your key direct reports, listen, admit that you have things to learn and value their experience, insights and suggestions. Your team will help you succeed, if you take the time to build personal relationships and set reasonable expectations. Importantly, celebrate the victories of the team. Should one of your team members not be willing to adapt to your leadership, you will want to make a change sooner rather than later.

I'm getting the feeling that my company thinks I'm "over the hill"

Companies can get this impression for many reasons. Maybe you are not exhibiting as high a level of energy as you have in the past, or you have become complacent about your work or appearance. Are you stuck in your thinking and less open to new ideas and ways of doing things? Maybe your results and contributions have not been quite as strong as they were previously or relative to others. Maybe you have not kept up in developing your skill sets or staying current with the trends and developments in your job function. Maybe your organization has become heavily populated with younger and more technology-literate executives, and the culture is changing. Maybe you have simply become too expensive.

Feeling out of touch or out-of-date is an uncomfortable position, no doubt. You may be receiving subtle signals such as being passed over for a promotion. You notice that you are not being invited to meetings where you used to be included or that you are not copied on emails. Maybe you now find yourself with reduced funding for your activities, personal training or development. Maybe you've recently been passed over for another position because the company feels that you are over qualified. Take the necessary time to understand the real issues behind this shift.

What can you do to try and refute or delay perceptions that you are over the hill? Maintain a high level of energy, dress the part, and become more tech savvy. Focus your time on activities and projects that have a visible and significant contribution to the business and let others see how your skills, experience, and results continue to add value. Be enthusiastic and positive. Continue to build internal relationships. Communicate that you would like to be with the company for the long-term, and reaffirm your commitment to the organization. Speak with

> Maintain a high level of energy, dress the part, and become more tech savvy.

other mature executives in the company and learn how they have stayed relevant. Under no circumstances, no matter how frustrated you are, should you even breathe the "R" word: retirement. Rumors start and spread very quickly. Do not stoke that fire.

If you believe that the issues are too entrenched and that perception is not likely to change, don't wait for the company to ask for your resignation. Begin looking for more accepting environments and cultures. This may mean looking at smaller companies where your experience, training, credibility and contacts can be put to better use.

I have lost all perspective on work-life balance

The greatest risk in this scenario is burnout. I went through this once during my career. It can take a year or more to re-establish the enthusiasm, energy and passion that you previously felt for your work. There is a distinction between working hard, which many people do, and making work an unhealthy, single-minded obsession. The other risk is the loss of objectivity and ability to step back and have a refreshed and broader perspective about your job and your business—to think on a higher plain, strategically. Additionally, personal relationships can become frayed. Marriages can fall apart and family members can feel that you are not there for them. Many severe workaholics sacrifice, at least in the short-term, those things that ultimately lead to a fully lived, rich and multi-dimensional existence. Without a range of new and broader experiences their personal growth can become stifled.

Managing an out-of-kilter work-life balance depends on whether it is self-inflicted or the result of external pressures and/ or unrealistic expectations or insufficient staffing. Take time to step back from the day-to-day pressures. If you decide that the pressure is self-inflicted, recognize this and think about how this is affecting you and those around you. Ask yourself whether you are working hard or working smart. Maybe you have recently been promoted to a larger managerial role. Are you learning to relinquish responsibility and depend on your team, or do you still feel that you need to be involved in everything? Do you try and please everyone at the office or do you know when and how to say no? Are the expectations being placed on you unrealistic? If, so, have a respectful but frank discussion with your superior and simply explain that your plate is presently too full and that there may be a better way to get the task done elsewhere. If your team is not sufficiently staffed, make the case for an additional hire.

To avoid burnout, nurture relationships and activities outside the office that provide some weekly variety in your life. Understand what activities will allow you to burn off any stress and frustrations. Take an interest in things other than your job. We all have room to do so. It's a big world! Another tactic I have found effective is to schedule time-off on your calendar to travel someplace you've never been. Adventures are a great antidote for maintaining perspective and re-opening yourself to new experiences. At one point during my career, I took off to Utah for several months to ski. I will never regret doing this. Experiences like this allow me to remember how fun life is, meet a lot of new people, and return with a whole new perspective, refreshed and with a clearer focus on my career plans.

> Understand what activities will allow you to burn off any stress and frustrations. Take an interest in things other than your job.

Undoubtedly, there are many other unexpected challenges that professionals face during the course of their forty to fifty-year careers. The bottom line is that there is no education like adversity. We all face career challenges. No one is immune. The best of us look at these unexpected challenges as opportunities to learn, grow, and improve. The best of us keep a cool head, seek to understand the dynamics of what is occurring and how we could be impacted. Only then can we determine how we can most productively respond to the situation.

Key Chapter Takeaways

)) Don't react immediately or overreact to an unexpected challenge.

)) Seek first to understand the challenge and dynamics that have led to the situation.

)) Talk with others to obtain their input about the situation or suggestions for remedying the challenge.

)) Formulate the response that you believe is most appropriate and pressure-test this response with a trusted colleague before responding.

Notes:

9

Conclusion

Congratulations! You are on your way to becoming a more Proactive Executive. You now have an appreciation for:

- The critical importance of taking charge of your career
- The influence of supply and demand in the talent market on your career advancement
- The ten key components that impact the attractiveness of your executive profile
- Where you may be underdeveloped and how to improve those aspects of your profile.

I encourage you to periodically retake the EPAM self-diagnostic to ensure that the attractiveness of your executive profile continues to get stronger.

In the book, we also spent time reviewing the building blocks for managing your career, including:

- mounting an effective job search
- networking in a targeted fashion
- creating a compelling resume
- interviewing effectively
- cultivating references
- negotiating compensation
- selecting the right job
- executing effective industry transitions
- getting off to a strong start in a new role

Next, we heard from executives about the most important lessons they have learned throughout their careers as well as the best professional advice they have received. Finally, we reviewed a number of potential "What if…?" scenarios and explored suggestions for how to respond to such circumstances.

Now that you have a more well-rounded understanding and practical framework for effectively managing your career, the next step is up to you. Refer back to this book as your career proceeds, and refresh your professional efforts with the material it provides. Keep a copy of "The Proactive Executive Reminder List" (found at the back of the book) at your office, and another on your bathroom mirror. Keep another copy in your wallet.

Consciously follow the five steps and accompanying action items that are outlined in this book. You do not have to do all five steps at once. Select the action steps that are most likely to benefit you based on where you are currently in your career. Work on one to two action steps each week in a focused and conscious manner. Take a few minutes at the end of each week to assess your progress, how you are better, and where else you should focus attention and energy. Some people find it very helpful to put a rubber band on their wrist or a pebble in their front pocket as a reminder of the one or two key things they need to work on each week. If you do not find yourself thinking about this material, get a bigger pebble and put it in your back pocket!

> Select the action steps that are most likely to benefit you based on where you are currently in your career.

Don't wait. Start today. There is no one else who will do this for you. The progress you experience will be very satisfying and give you confidence. The dividends will be abundant. I am certain of this. I see these principles work every day in my executive coaching activities.

I wish you much success, happiness and satisfaction with your career in the coming years. If your journey is one bit smoother or quicker as a result of guidance provided in *The Proactive Executive*, then I have succeeded. Should we ever have the chance to meet or you care to drop me a note on my website—chrisnadherny.com— I'd be thrilled to hear how this book has assisted you. If there are additional topics that you would like to see included in future editions, please let me know. Should you wish to learn more about the seminars, workshops or selective one-on-one coaching I provide, my website is also a great place to connect with me.

Now, venture forth and optimize your career potential!

Notes:

The Proactive Executive Reminder List

Your professional profile is one of the most valuable assets you have. Managing your career proactively and thoughtfully will result in greater career advancement, more job satisfaction and enhanced earnings potential. Mismanagement of your career results in lost potential. Missteps can have detrimental repercussions that ripple through your career for years. Take this reminder list and put it somewhere where you can look at it daily. Tape a copy to your bathroom mirror, keep a copy in your wallet, and one at the office.

- Be proactive, deliberate and thoughtful in managing your career. No one else will do it for you.

- Position your professional profile in the market to take advantage of the laws of supply and demand for talent. Strive to position yourself in the High Demand/Limited Supply quadrant.

- As often as possible, place yourself in scenarios where you "fill a void" in a growing company or segment of the business. It will be easier to show accomplishments and get noticed.

- Understand your foundational strengths, which will become the backbone of your career. Seek roles that allow you to leverage these strengths.

- Identify your shortcomings and understand how to manage or improve on them.

- Network in an ongoing and targeted manner. While online networking is certainly one avenue, personal interaction is more impactful. The "human touch" makes a difference.

You can do this by phone or face-to-face. Make targeted networking a permanent part of your weekly activity.

- Build career allies. Extend yourself for other professionals and provide favors and assistance where ever and whenever you can. These professionals will remember you in a positive light. There may well come a day when you will need their assistance, want to have them as part of your team or require their cooperation.

- Cultivate references on an ongoing basis. Don't wait until the moment they are needed.

- Change jobs for opportunity, fit, and growth—not simply money.

- Build strong internal working relationships at the companies for which you work.

- Make smart, strategic and well-informed career moves. Ask yourself, "What is the best that could happen? What is the worst? How does this move put me closer to my career objective? What are the career downsides, if the worst occurs?"

- Build and cherish your reputation every day.

- Do you job exceptionally well!

Acknowledgements

Writing this book would not have been possible without the opportunity to work with so many wonderful clients, senior executives and colleagues during my 30 years with Spencer Stuart. All of those interactions shaped my writing of *The Proactive Executive*. I watched the careers of many of these executives unfold.

I would not have even entered the search business, if it weren't for a call in 1985 from the managing director of the Spencer Stuart Chicago office, Jim Drury. Jim not only convinced me to join the firm, but he believed in me and supported me throughout my early career in executive search.

Curt Fee, a now retired colleague, offered invaluable early mentoring. Tom Hardy, one of the early Consumer Goods Practice leaders, provided the initial funding to build the Direct Marketing Practice within Spencer Stuart—a project that I had proposed and spearheaded. Tom's belief in my proposal allowed me to develop a viable business and identity within the firm, and set the stage for launching the Internet Practice with Jim Citrin. Jim has been a thought leader within Spencer Stuart for many years and presently leads the firm's CEO practice.

David Daniel, the firm's CEO during the critical years when we expanded the Internet Practice, lent his support for our initiatives. Many other colleagues have championed these efforts including, but not limited to, Kevin Connelly (the firm's CEO these last five years), Kristin Bradley (my always reliable and trusted research associate), Greg Welch (who I teamed with on many searches), Tim McNary and Anne Schmidt (who partnered with me over the years on "leadership" intellectual capital).

The initial seed for *The Proactive Executive* was a very short summary of important career guidance that I drafted for my sons, Weston and Matthew. This effort grew as I began thinking about all the careers I'd observed and influenced over the years. I was unable to find any career books that provided a focused, practical and complete circumnavigation of effective career management. Having never published a book, I decided that this would be a new challenge and opportunity to not only help my grown sons, but countless others.

Special acknowledgement goes to a long-time client, Rick Marcantonio, whose initial enthusiastic response to my early manuscript drove me onward. "This is gold," he told me. "I'll buy 12 copies right now!" I greatly value Rick's friendship and loyalty. Over the years, I conducted close to 40 searches for him, and watched as he progressed from Keebler to Ecolab to G&K Services and rose into top leadership roles.

I also want to express my thanks to the individuals I interviewed for the "Lessons Learned from Successful Executives" chapter of this book. Since I promised you all semi-anonymity, I won't thank you each by name. However, know that your input and stories were an invaluable addition to the book.

Additionally, Tom Collinger at Northwestern's Medill School provided valuable feedback on the front end of this project. Cathryn Taylor, president of the Wharton Club of Chicago, embraced the concept for a broader vision of career planning and management. She challenged me to develop a "How to Optimize Your Career" seminar series and workshop, which we have now launched with terrific success. This seminar, discussion series and a workshops are presently being expanded. This activity, in turn, led to one-on-one coaching with executives needing more intensive assistance. The direct and positive impact of this coaching has been especially satisfying. Cathryn also introduced me to Melissa Wilson of Networlding, and she in turn introduced me to Kathy Meis of Bublish. Kathy has been a godsend in this effort! She has been my editor, publisher, distributor and educator in this endeavor… providing timely insight and advice. I can't recommend her services highly enough. A special thanks also goes to Wally Scott, a long time professor at Northwestern's Kellogg Business School and a family friend. Wally took the time to review the very early manuscript in great and thoughtful detail and made many, many helpful suggestions.

Last, but certainly number one on my list, I want to thank the love of my life, Yan Shields. Her sunny disposition and good spirit are very special. Yan showed tremendous patience and under-standing while I was focused on the completion of this book.

About the Author

││││

Chris Nadherny is a former executive search consultant, who worked with Spencer Stuart's Chicago office for 30 years. He now coaches mid-career and senior executives about how to effectively manage their careers, improve their marketability and optimize their long-term potential. His early career was in telecommunications and then consumer marketing with PepsiCo and Johnson & Johnson. During his tenure with Spencer Stuart as a consultant, partner, and practice leader, Chris also served as Chair of the Partner Development Committee and sat on the Board Nominating Committee. Additionally, he co-founded and led Spencer Stuart's Global Digital Practice.

Chris has conducted more than 700 national search assignments for a wide range of small, mid-sized, large and global client organizations, both public and privately held. These assignments were across a full range of industries and leadership functions at levels ranging from vice president through chief executive officer and board director roles. Former clients include consumer goods and service firms, multi-channel retailers, hospitality and leisure companies, pure-play internet businesses, health-care companies, private equity firms, and business-to-business product and service companies.

Since retiring from Spencer Stuart in 2015, Chris has developed a career- management consultancy focused on helping executives reach their desired career objectives. His career guidebook, *The Proactive Executive*, encapsulates insights from his interaction with thousands of successful executives throughout his career. Chris is creator of a Career Management Seminar Series and Workshop entitled "How to Optimize Your Career" for aspiring and senior executives. These workshops are conducted in small group settings for 6-12 professionals and in a larger seminar format for groups of 30 to 70 executives.

A graduate of Union College in New York, Chris received his M.B.A. from the Wharton School of Business. In addition to managing his consultancy, he is a Senior Advisor to GVG Capital, a private equity firm focused on digital, ecommerce and multi-channel retail.

Made in the USA
Coppell, TX
06 September 2020

36032813R10125